The Voices of War

Perception in Communication

THE VOICES OF WAR

EDITED BY *James Shokoff*

*State University College of New York
at Fredonia*

JOHN WILEY & SONS, INC.

NEW YORK · LONDON · SYDNEY · TORONTO

Library of Congress Catalogue Card Number: 74-37367

ISBN 0-471-78791-4

Printed in the United States of America.

10 9 8 7 6 5 4 3 2 1

Series Preface

"Perception in Communication" is a series of brief topical readers presenting a collection of expository prose, verse, fiction, drama, and nonverbal media for the student of composition. No restrictive framework has been imposed on any of the volumes. If a common framework exists, it stems from the editors' emphasis on the principle of comparison and contrast and their mutual desire to make the questions and exercises participatory. The questions are focused on themes and matters of rhetorical technique that will provoke discussion between instructor and student in responses to the authors and editors.

Experience demonstrates that a student tends to write better when a timely, substantial subject engages his interest, or when the subject is elaborated and reviewed in a variety of modes of communication. Although the major emphasis of this series is on written communication, there are also a number of multimedia projects such as collages, comic routines, poems, dramatic productions, films, pictorial essays, posters, songs, and tapes. The editors use this multimedia material in such a manner that they are very definitely assignments in composition.

By acknowledging several modes of communication and encouraging experimentation in more than one, the editors recognize the heterogeneity of today's college audience and its various commitments, concerns, goals, and needs. It is the editors' belief that presenting these various modes of communication will engage not only the reader's mind but also his sensory perception.

CHARLES SANDERS

University of Illinois at Urbana

Preface

A famed general once said, "War is Hell," and few people have ever had reason to dispute him.[1] If there is one point on which all mankind may agree, it is the hatred of warfare and of the terror, pestilence, and horror that are its offspring. Yet wars go on. Peace on earth is a dream we have never fully realized and, what is more, with every generation our wars have become more frightful—wider in their destruction and more deadly to more people. The once unthinkable carnage of the American Civil War was superseded by the bloody trenches of 1918 in France, which yielded in gore to Dachau and Hiroshima where civilians rather than soldiers became the principal victims. Finally we have encountered a civilized madness called limited warfare in which nations like Korea, Hungary, Czechoslovakia, and Vietnam become asylums for organized dehumanization and brutality.

The chief aim of this book is to see the realities of war as they are seen by those who know war intimately—soldiers in the front lines, civilians trapped by the mighty forces around them, generals, philosphers, and leaders. To each, war is a very special, personal thing. To the bombardeer it is a job that must be done and done

---

[1] General William Tecumseh Sherman actually said, on August 11, 1880 at Columbus, Ohio, "There is many a boy here today who looks on war as all glory, but, boys, it is all hell." History has made his words more pithy.

well; to the man in the trenches it is a contest for survival. To the woman who has lost a son or husband it is either a glorious or cruel thief; to the victim at Dubno it is a nightmare from which the only awakening is death. To the commander or to the thinker, it is a problem that one must solve, each in his own way. Brought together, these views do not total a definition of war, but they do make a start toward understanding it and toward attempting to answer the seemingly eternal questions: *Why War?* and *How can we avoid war?*

A second objective of this book is to use war as a subject to which students can commit themselves in their efforts to develop effective means of expression and communication. As far as writing is concerned, a premise underlying the study questions and the composition assignments that call for expository or narrative prose is that the author's persona or rhetorical stance is basic to his craft. Our daily lives offer a supportive analogy to this premise. Each of us, every day, plays many roles—the student in the classroom, the athlete in the gym, the romancer on the phone with a pretty girl, or the son at home arguing across the generation gap. The stance we take, the voice we use, and the face we wear are likely to be different in each of these situations, but this does not mean that we are being hypocritical or dishonest. Instead, when we choose a stance, or voice, or face, we are drawing upon the complexity of our being. We are all of these things, although never all at once. The aspect we choose at any given time becomes a personal essay to do as best we can the job we want to get done.

The process of writing requires a similar choice of role on the part of the writer. In this book, each author looks at war from a particular stance or point of view. The battle to the general is not the same battle that the private describes, nor does the death of a soldier have the same meaning to his killer as it does to his mother or his widow. The identity of the persona, the voice behind the piece of writing, determines to a great extent both how the persona sees war and what his attitude toward war is.

Understanding the function of the persona or rhetorical stance is an important step in developing a flexible and effective style of writing. Once a writer is aware of who he is as an author and, if he can visualize it, who his audience is, his rhetorical choices—of words, details, examples, and the like—become relatively easy, because he has given himself a frame the limits of which he may not violate. He has done what virtually every writing teacher demands of his students: he has narrowed his topic by looking at it from a specific point of view.

But it is increasingly true in our post-McLuhan world that writing is not the only effective means of communication. The power of the cinema, for example, is evident when one realizes how much information can be packed into a good one-minute film and, moreover, how well an audience retains that information. Frequently, a piece of visual art—a painting, a collage, or a photograph—will validate anew the ancient axiom about the worth of one picture. Sound, too—the human voice, abstract sounds, an aural collage—can communicate with great strength when the composer has chosen and ordered his material sensitively. Recognition of the fact that college composition today can profitably include more than expository and narrative writing has prompted the nonverbal and mixed-media suggestions for composition throughout this book.

Finally, by joining a broad approach to the process of composition with an anatomy of war, this book will help students not only to develop competence in the expression of their ideas but to become concerned, knowledgeable citizens and potential forces of change in a world that no longer can afford to accept the inevitability of war.

JAMES SHOKOFF

ACKNOWLEDGMENTS

I am grateful for the assistance, advice, and encouragement of many people. Some of them are Charles Sanders, the general editor of this series; Thomas O. Gay, of Wiley; Houston Peterson, Professor Emeritus of Rutgers University; Dennis Dalton of Barnard College; John Harrington of the University of Massachusetts; Marie Harrington; Ruth Shokoff; Elisa Shokoff; and Christopher Shokoff.

J. S.

Contents

The Voices of War

Part One

WAR AT THE
FRONT

"Once more unto the breach, dear friends, once more;
Or close the wall up with our English dead."

—HENRY V (III, i)

1. *Picnic on the Battlefield*

FERNANDO ARRABAL

CHARACTERS

ZAPO, *a soldier*
MONSIEUR TÉPAN, *the soldier's father*
MADAME TÉPAN, *the soldier's mother*
ZÉPO, *an enemy soldier*
FIRST CORPSMAN
SECOND CORPSMAN

Scene: *A battlefield. Barbed wire stretches from one end of the stage to the other, with sandbags piled against it.*
Battle is in full swing. We hear bombs bursting, rifle shots and machine-gun fire.
Alone on stage, hidden flat on his belly among the sandbags, ZAPO *is very frightened.*
The fighting stops. Silence.
From a knitting-bag, ZAPO *takes out a ball of wool, knitting needles, and starts knitting a sweater that is already quite well along. The field telephone beside him suddenly rings.*
ZAPO. Hello . . . hello . . . yes, sir, Captain. . . . Yes, this is the

Reprinted by permission of Grove Press, Inc. Translated from the French by Barbara Wright. These translations copyright © 1967 by Calder and Boyars Ltd., London.

sentry in Section 47. . . . Nothing new, Captain. . . . Excuse me, Captain, when are we going to start fighting again? . . . And what am I supposed to do with the grenades? Should I send them on up front or to the rear? . . . Don't get annoyed, I didn't say that to upset you. . . . And, Captain, I'm really feeling pretty lonesome. Couldn't you send me a companion out here? . . . Even the goat. (*Evidently the Captain gives him a good dressing down.*) Yet sir, Captain, yes sir! (ZAPO *hangs up. We hear him grumbling to himself. Silence.*)

[*Enter* MONSIEUR *and* MADAME TÉPAN, *carrying baskets as though they are off on a picnic. Their son, who is sitting with his back turned, does not see them arriving.*]

M. TÉPAN (*ceremoniously*). My boy, get up and kiss your mother on the forehead.

[*Taken by surprise,* ZAPO *gets up and, with a great deal of respect, gives his mother a kiss on the forehead. He is about to speak, but his father beats him to it.*]

Now give *me* a kiss.

ZAPO. My dear sweet parents, how did you ever dare come all the way out to a dangerous spot like this? You must leave here right away.

M. TÉPAN. Are you trying to tell your father what war and danger are all about? For me, all this is only a game. How many times do you think I've jumped off the subway while it was still moving?

MME. TÉPAN. We thought you were probably bored, so we came to pay you a little visit. After all, this war business must get pretty tiresome.

ZAPO. It all depends.

M. TÉPAN. I know perfectly well what goes on. In the beginning, it's all new and exciting. You enjoy the killing and throwing grenades and wearing a helmet; it's quite the thing, but you end up bored as hell. In my day, you'd have really seen something. Wars were a lot livelier, much more colorful. And then best of all, there were horses, lots of horses. It was a real pleasure: if the captain said "Attack!" before you could shake a stick we were all assembled on horseback in our red uniforms. That was something to see. And then we'd go galloping forward, sword in hand, and suddenly find ourselves hard against the enemy. And they'd be at their finest too, with their horses —there were always loads and loads of beautifully round-bottomed horses and their polished boots, and their green uniforms.

MME. TÉPAN. No, the enemy uniform wasn't green. It was blue. I remember perfectly well it was blue.

M. TÉPAN. And I say it was green.

MME. TÉPAN. When I was little I went out on the balcony any number of times to watch the battle, and I'd say to the little boy next door, "I'll bet you a gumdrop the Blues win." And the Blues were our enemies.

M. TÉPAN. All right, so you win.

MME. TÉPAN. I always loved battles. When I was little, I always said that when I grew up I wanted to be a Colonel in the Dragoons. But Mama didn't want me to. You know what a stickler she is.

M. TÉPAN. Your mother's a real nincompoop.

ZAPO. Forgive me, but you've got to leave. You can't go walking into a war when you're not a soldier.

M. TÉPAN. I don't give a damn. We're here to have a picnic with you in the country and spend a nice Sunday.

MME. TÉPAN. I even made a lovely meal. Sausage, hard-boiled eggs, I know how much you like them! Ham sandwiches, red wine, some salad and some little cakes.

ZAPO. O.K., we'll do whatever you say. But if the Captain comes along he'll throw a fit. Plus the fact that he doesn't go for the idea of visiting the battlefront. He keeps telling us: "War calls for discipline and grenades, but no visits."

M. TÉPAN. Don't you worry about it, I'll have a few words with your Captain.

ZAPO. And what if we have to start fighting again?

M. TÉPAN. You think that scares me, I've seen worse. Now if it was only cavalry battles! Times have changed, that's something you don't understand. (*A pause.*) We came on motorcycle. Nobody said anything.

ZAPO. They probably thought you were arbitrators.

M. TÉPAN. We did have some trouble getting through, though. With all those jeeps and tanks.

MME. TÉPAN. And the very minute we arrived, you remember that bottleneck because of the cannon?

M. TÉPAN. During wartime, you've got to be prepared for anything. Everybody knows that.

MME. TÉPAN. Well now, we're ready to start eating.

M. TÉPAN.   Right you are, I could eat a horse. It's the smell of gun-powder that does it.

MME. TÉPAN.   We'll eat sitting down on the blanket.

ZAPO.   All right to eat with my rifle?

MME. TÉPAN.   Let your rifle alone. It's bad manners to bring your rifle to the table. (*A pause.*) Why, child, you're filthy as a little pig. How did you manage to get in such a mess? Let's see your hands.

ZAPO.   (*Ashamed, he shows them.*) I had to crawl along the ground during maneuvers.

MME. TÉPAN.   How about your ears?

ZAPO.   I washed them this morning.

MME. TÉPAN.   That should do then. Now how about your teeth? (*He shows them.*) Very good. Now who's going to give his little boy a great big kiss for brushing his teeth so nicely? (*To her husband.*) Well, give your son a kiss for brushing his teeth so nicely. (M. TÉPAN *gives his son a kiss.*) Because, you know, one thing I just won't allow is not washing, and blaming it on the war.

ZAPO.   Yes, Mama
    [*They eat.*]

M. TÉPAN.   Well, my boy, have you been keeping up a good shooting score?

ZAPO.   When?

M. TÉPAN.   Why, the last few days.

ZAPO.   Where?

M. TÉPAN.   Right here and now. After all, you *are* fighting a war.

ZAPO.   No, no great shakes. I haven't kept up a very good score. Practically no bull's-eyes.

M. TÉPAN.   Well, what have you been scoring best with in your shooting, enemy horses or soldiers?

ZAPO.   No, no horses. There aren't any horses any more.

M. TÉPAN.   Well, soldiers then?

ZAPO.   Could be.

M. TÉPAN.   Could be? Aren't you sure?

ZAPO.   It's just that I . . . I fire without taking aim (*a pause*) and when I fire I say an *Our Father* for the guy I shot.

M. TÉPAN.   You've got to show more courage. Like your father.

MME. TÉPAN.   I'm going to put a record on the phonograph. (*She puts on a record: a Spanish pasodoble. Sitting on the ground, they all three listen.*)

M. TÉPAN. Now that's real music. Yes, ma'am. I tell you. *Olé!*
[*As the music continues, an enemy soldier,* ZÉPO *enters. He is dressed like* ZAPO. *Only the color of his uniform is different.* ZÉPO *wears green;* ZAPO *wears gray.*
Standing unseen behind the family, his mouth agape, ZÉPO *listens to the music. The record comes to an end.* ZAPO, *getting up, spots* ZÉPO. *Both raise their hands in the air, while* M. *and* MME. TÉPAN *look at them, startled.*]
M. TÉPAN. What's going on?
[ZAPO *seems about to act, but hesitates. Then, very decisively, he points his rifle at* ZÉPO.]
ZAPO. Hands up!
[ZÉPO, *more terrified than ever, raises his hands still higher.* ZAPO *doesn't know what to do. All of a sudden, he hurriedly runs toward* ZÉPO *and taps him gently on the shoulder, saying*]
ZAPO. You're it! (*Pleased as punch, to his father.*) There you are! A prisoner!
M. TÉPAN. That's fine. Now what are you going to do with him?
ZAPO. I don't know. But could be they'll make me a corporal.
M. TÉPAN. In the meantime, tie him up.
ZAPO. Tie him up? What for?
M. TÉPAN. That's what you do with prisoners, you tie 'em up!
ZAPO. How?
M. TÉPAN. By his hands.
MME. TÉPAN. Oh yes, you've definitely got to tie his hands. That's the way I've always seen it done.
ZAPO. All right. (*To the prisoner.*) Please put your hands together.
ZÉPO. Don't do it too hard.
ZAPO. Oh, no.
ZÉPO. Ouch! You're hurting me.
M. TÉPAN. Come on now, don't mistreat your prisoner.
MME. TÉPAN. Is that the way I brought you up? Haven't I told you over and over again that you've got to be considerate of your fellow man?
ZAPO. I didn't do it on purpose. (*To* ZÉPO.) Does it hurt the way it is now?
ZÉPO. No, like this it doesn't hurt.
M. TÉPAN. Speak right up and tell him if it does. Just pretend we're not here.
ZÉPO. This way it's O.K.
M. TÉPAN. Now his feet.

ZAPO. His feet too? How long does this go on?

M. TÉPAN. Didn't they teach you the rules?

ZAPO. Sure.

M. TÉPAN. Well?

ZAPO (*to* ZÉPO, *very politely*). Would you kindly be good enough to please sit down on the ground?

ZÉPO. All right, but don't hurt me.

MME. TÉPAN. See! Now he's taking a dislike to you.

ZAPO. No. No he's not. I'm not hurting you, am I?

ZÉPO. No, this is fine.

ZAPO (*out of nowhere*). Papa, suppose you took a snapshot with the prisoner down there on the ground and me standing with my foot on his stomach?

M. TÉPAN. Say, yes! That'll look classy.

ZÉPO. Oh, no you don't. Not that.

MME. TÉPAN. Let him. Don't be so stubborn.

ZÉPO. No. I said no and mean no.

MME. TÉPAN. Just a little old snip of a snapshot. What difference could that possibly make to you? Then we could put it in the dining room right next to the Lifesaving Certificate my husband got thirteen years ago.

ZÉPO. No, you'll never talk me into it.

ZAPO. But why should you refuse?

ZÉPO. I've got a fiancée. And if she ever sees the snapshot, she'll say I don't know how to fight a war.

ZAPO. No, all you have to do is tell her it isn't you at all, it's a panther.

MME. TÉPAN. C'mon, say yes.

ZÉPO. All right, but I'm only doing it to please you.

ZAPO. Stretch all the way out.

[ZÉPO *stretches all the way out.* ZAPO *puts one foot on his stomach and grabs his rifle with a military air.*]

MME. TÉPAN. Throw your chest out more.

ZAPO. Like this?

MME. TÉPAN. Yes, that's it. Don't breathe.

M. TÉPAN. Make like a hero.

ZAPO. How do you mean a hero, like this?

M. TÉPAN. It's a cinch. Make like the butcher when he was telling us what a lady-killer he is.

ZAPO. Like so?

M. TÉPAN. Yes, that's it.

MME. TÉPAN.   Just be sure your chest is puffed way out, and don't breathe.

ZÉPO.   Are you about finished?

M. TÉPAN.   Have a little patience. One . . . two . . . three.

ZAPO.   I hope I'll come out all right.

MME. TÉPAN.   Oh yes, you looked very military.

M. TÉPAN.   You were fine.

MME. TÉPAN.   That makes me want to have my picture taken, too.

M. TÉPAN.   Now there's a good idea.

ZAPO.   All right. I'll take it if you want me to.

MME. TÉPAN.   Give me your helmet so I'll look like a soldier.

ZÉPO.   I don't want any more pictures. Even one was too much.

ZAPO.   Don't feel that way. Come right down to it, what difference could it make?

ZÉPO.   That's my final say.

M. TÉPAN   (*to his wife*). Don't push him. Prisoners are always very touchy. If we keep it up, he'll get mad and spoil all our fun.

ZAPO.   Well now, what are we going to do with him?

MME. TÉPAN.   We could ask him to eat with us. What do you think?

M. TÉPAN.   I don't see any reason why not.

ZAPO (*to* ZÉPO).   All right then, how'd you like to eat with us?

ZÉPO.   Uh . . .

M. TÉPAN.   We brought along a nice bottle of wine.

ZÉPO.   Well, in that case O.K.

MME. TÉPAN.   Make yourself right at home. Don't be afraid to ask for things.

ZÉPO.   Fine.

M. TÉPAN.   Well now, how about you, have you been keeping up a good shooting score?

ZÉPO.   When?

M. TÉPAN.   Why, the last few days.

ZÉPO.   Where?

M. TÉPAN.   Right here and now. After all, you *are* fighting a war.

ZÉPO.   No, no great shakes. I haven't kept up a very good score. Practically no bull's-eyes.

M. TÉPAN.   Well, what have you been scoring best with in your shooting, enemy horses or soldiers?

ZÉPO.   No, no horses. There aren't any horses any more.

M. TÉPAN.   Well, soldiers then?

ZÉPO.   Could be.

M. TÉPAN.   Could be? Aren't you sure?

ZÉPO.   It's just that I . . . I fire without taking aim (*a pause*) and when I fire I say a *Hail Mary* for the guy I shot.

ZAPO.   A *Hail Mary?* I'd have thought you'd say an *Our Father.*

ZÉPO.   No. Always a *Hail Mary.* (*A pause.*) It's shorter.

M. TÉPAN.   Come, my boy, you have to be courageous.

MME. TÉPAN (*to* ZÉPO). If you like, we can untie you.

ZÉPO.   No, leave me this way. It doesn't matter.

M TÉPAN.   You're not going to start putting on airs with us? If you want us to untie you, just say the word.

MME. TÉPAN.   Please feel free.

ZÉPO.   Well, if you really mean it, untie my feet. But it's just to please you people.

M. TÉPAN.   Zapo, untie him.

[ZAPO *unties him.*]

MME. TÉPAN.   Well now, feel better?

ZÉPO.   Sure do. But listen, maybe I'm causing you too much trouble.

M. TÉPAN.   Not at all. Make yourself right at home. And if you want us to undo your hands, just say so.

ZÉPO.   No, not my hands, too. I don't want to overdo it.

M. TÉPAN.   Not at all, my boy, not at all. I tell you, you don't disturb us one bit.

ZÉPO.   All right, go ahead and untie my hands then. But just while we eat, huh? I don't want you to think when you give me an inch I'm going to take a mile.

M. TÉPAN.   Untie his hands, sonny.

MME. TÉPAN.   Well, since our honorable prisoner is so nice, we're going to have a lovely day out here in the country.

ZÉPO.   Don't call me "honorable" prisoner. Just say "prisoner" plain and simple.

MME. TÉPAN.   You're sure that won't make you feel bad?

ZÉPO.   No, not at all.

M. TÉPAN.   Well, you're certainly unpretentious, anyway.

[*Sound of airplanes.*]

ZAPO.   Airplanes. They're going to bomb us for sure.

[ZAPO *and* ZÉPO *dive for the sandbags and hide.*]

ZAPO (*to his parents*).   Run for cover! The bombs are going to land right on you.

[*The sound of the planes drowns out everything. Immediately bombs start falling. Shells explode nearby. Deafening racket.* ZAPO *and* ZÉPO *are crouching among the sandbags.* M. TÉPAN *goes on calmly talking to his wife, who answers him with equal*

calm. *Because of the bombardment we cannot hear their con-*
versation.

MME. TÉPAN *heads for one of the picnic baskets, from which*
she takes an umbrella. She opens it. The TÉPANS *take shelter*
under the umbrella as though it were raining. Standing there,
they shift from one foot to the other, in rhythm, all the while
discussing personal matters. The bombardment continues. At
last, the airplanes take off. Silence.

M. TÉPAN *stretches one arm out from under the umbrella to make*
certain there is no longer anything coming down from the sky.]

M. TÉPAN.   You can close your umbrella now.

[MME. TÉPAN *closes it. Together they go over to their son and*
prod him on the behind a couple of times with the umbrella.]

M. TÉPAN.   All right, come on out. The bombing's over.

[ZAPO *and* ZÉPO *come out of their hiding place.*]

ZAPO.   They didn't get you?

M. TÉPAN.   You don't expect anything to happen to your father, do
you? (*Proudly.*) Little bombs like that? Don't make me laugh.
[*From the left, a pair of Red Cross* CORPSMEN *enter, carrying*
a stretcher.]

FIRST CORPSMAN.   Any bodies?

ZAPO.   No, none here.

FIRST CORPSMAN.   You're sure you took a good look?

ZAPO.   Absolutely.

FIRST CORPSMAN.   And there's not one single body?

ZAPO.   Didn't I just say so?

FIRST CORPSMAN.   Not even someone wounded?

ZAPO.   Not even.

SECOND CORPSMAN.   Well, we're really up the creek! (*To* ZAPO,
persuasively.) Take a good look all around here, see if you
don't turn up a stiff someplace.

FIRST CORPSMAN.   Don't press the issue. They told you once and for
all there aren't any.

SECOND CORPSMAN.   What a lousy deal!

ZAPO.   I'm really very sorry. I swear I didn't plan it that way.

SECOND CORPSMAN.   That's what they all say. That there aren't any
corpses, and that they didn't plan it that way.

FIRST CORPSMAN.   So let the man alone!

M. TÉPAN (*obligingly*).   If we can help you at all, we'd be delighted to. At your service.

SECOND CORPSMAN. Well, I don't know. If we keep on like this, I really don't know what the Captain's going to say to us.

M. TÉPAN. What seems to be the trouble?

SECOND CORPSMAN. Just that the others are all getting sore wrists carrying out the dead and wounded, while we still haven't come up with anything. And it's not because we haven't been looking.

M. TÉPAN. I see. That really is a bore. (*To* ZAPO.) You're quite sure there are no corpses?

ZAPO. Obviously, Papa.

M. TÉPAN. You looked under the sandbags?

ZAPO. Yes, Papa.

M. TÉPAN (*angrily*). Why don't you come right out and say you don't want to have any part in helping these good gentlemen?

FIRST CORPSMAN. Don't jump on him like that. Leave him alone. We'll just hope we have better luck in some other trench where maybe everybody'll be dead.

M. TÉPAN. I'd be delighted for you.

MME. TÉPAN. So would I. Nothing pleases me more than to see people who take their work seriously.

M. TÉPAN. (*Indignantly, to anyone within hearing*). Well, isn't anyone going to do anything for these gentlemen?

ZAPO. If it was up to me, it'd be good as done.

ZÉPO. Same here.

M. TÉPAN. Look here now, isn't one of you at least wounded?

ZAPO (*ashamed*). No, not me.

M. TÉPAN (*to* ZÉPO). What about you?

ZÉPO (*ashamed*). Me either. I never was lucky.

MME. TÉPAN (*delighted*). I just remembered! This morning, while I was peeling onions, I cut my finger. How's that?

M. TÉPAN. Why of course! (*Really in the swing of things.*) They'll put you on the stretcher and carry you right off!

FIRST CORPSMAN. Sorry, it's no good. Women don't count.

M. TÉPAN. Well, that didn't get us anywhere.

FIRST CORPSMAN. It doesn't matter.

SECOND CORPSMAN. Maybe we can get our fill in the other trenches. (*They start to go off.*)

M. TÉPAN. Don't you worry, if we find a corpse, we'll hang onto it for you. There's not a chance we'd give it to anybody but you.

SECOND CORPSMAN. Thank you very much, sir.

M. TÉPAN. It's nothing, my boy. It's the very least I could do.

[*The* CORPSMEN *make their goodbyes. All four of the others reply in kind. The* CORPSMEN *exit.*]

MME. TÉPAN. That's what's so pleasant about spending Sunday out in the battlefield. You always run into such nice folks. (*A pause.*) Come to think of it, why is it you're enemies?

ZÉPO. I don't know. I'm not too well educated.

MME. TÉPAN. I mean is it from birth, or did you become enemies after?

ZÉPO. I don't know. I don't know a thing about it.

M. TÉPAN. Well then, how did you come to go to war?

ZÉPO. One day I was home fixing my mother's iron and a man came by and said to me: "Are you Zépo?" . . . "Yes." . . . "Good, you've got to go to war." So I asked him, "What war?" And he said to me: "Don't you read the newspapers? You *are* a hick!" So I told him yes I did, but not all that war stuff . . .

ZAPO. That's just what happened to me; exactly what happened to me.

M. TÉPAN. Sure, they came after you, too.

MME. TÉPAN. No, it's not the same. You weren't fixing the iron that day, you were repairing the car.

M. TÉPAN. I was talking about the rest of it. (*To* ZÉPO.) Go on. Then what happened?

ZÉPO. Well, then I told him that I had a fiancée, and if I didn't take her to the movies on Sunday, she wouldn't know what to do with herself. He said that that didn't matter.

ZAPO. Same as me. Exactly the same as me.

ZÉPO. Well, then my father came down and he said I couldn't go to war because I didn't have a horse.

ZAPO. Like my father said.

ZÉPO. The man said they didn't use horses any more, and I asked him if I could take along my fiancée. He said no. Then I asked him could I take along my aunt to make me custard every Thursday. I like custard.

MME. TÉPAN (*realizing that she has forgotten something*). Oh! The custard!

ZÉPO. Again he said no.

ZAPO. The way he did to me.

ZÉPO. And ever since then, here I am, nearly always all alone in the trench here.

MME. TÉPAN. As long as you're so much alike, and both so bored,

I think you and your honorable prisoner might play together this afternoon.

ZAPO. Oh no, Mama! I'm too scared. He's an enemy.

M. TÉPAN. Oh come on now, don't be scared.

ZAPO. If you knew what the general told us about the enemy.

MME. TÉPAN. What did he tell you?

ZAPO. He said the enemy soldiers are very mean. When they take prisoners, they put pebbles in their socks so it hurts when they walk.

MME. TÉPAN. How horrible! What savages!

M. TÉPAN (*indignantly, to* ZÉPO). Aren't you ashamed to be part of an army of criminals?

ZÉPO. I didn't do anything. I'm not mad at anybody.

MME. TÉPAN. He's trying to put one over on us, acting like a little saint.

M. TÉPAN. We should never have untied him. Probably all we have to do is have our backs turned for him to go putting pebbles in our socks.

ZÉPO. Don't be so mean to me.

M. TÉPAN. How do you expect us to be? I'm shocked. I know just what I'm going to do. I'm going to find the Captain and ask him to let me go into battle.

ZAPO. He won't let you. You're too old.

M. TÉPAN. Well then I'll go buy a horse and a saber and I'll go to war on my own.

ZÉPO. Please, madame, don't treat me like this. Besides, I was just going to tell you, *our* general said the same thing about you people.

MME. TÉPAN. How could he dare tell such a lie?

ZAPO. The very same thing, honest?

ZÉPO. Yes, the very same thing.

M. TÉPAN. Maybe it's the same one who talked to both of you.

MME. TÉPAN. Well, if it is the same general, the least he could do is use a different speech. Imagine telling everybody the same thing.

M. TÉPAN (*to* ZÉPO, *changing his tone*). Can I fill your glass again?

MME. TÉPAN. I hope you enjoyed our little lunch.

M. TÉPAN. It was better than last Sunday, anyway.

ZÉPO. What happened then?

M. TÉPAN. Well, we went out to the country and laid all our chow out on the blanket. While we had our backs turned, a cow came along and ate the whole lunch, including the napkins.

ZÉPO.   What a glutton, that cow!

M. TÉPAN.   Yes, but then to get even, we ate the cow.

[*They laugh.*]

ZAPO (*to* ZÉPO).   I bet they weren't hungry after that.

M. TÉPAN.   To your health!

[*They all drink.*]

MME. TÉPAN (*to* ZÉPO).   Tell me something, what do you do for amusement in the trenches?

ZÉPO.   Just to pass the time and keep myself amused, I take odds and ends of rags and make little flowers out of them. See, I get bored a lot.

MME. TÉPAN.   And what do you do with these rag flowers?

ZÉPO.   At first I used to send them to my fiancée, but one day she told me that the cellar and the greenhouse were already filled with them, that she didn't know what to do with them any more, and would I mind sending her something else for a change?

MME. TÉPAN.   And what did you do?

ZÉPO.   I tried learning something else, but I couldn't do it. So, to pass the time, I just go on making my rag flowers.

MME. TÉPAN.   And then do you throw them away?

ZÉPO.   No, now I've found a way to make use of them: I furnish one flower for each of my buddies who dies. That way, I know that even if I make a whole lot, there'll never be enough.

M. TÉPAN.   You found a good way out.

ZÉPO (*timidly*). Yes.

ZAPO.   Well, you know what I do so's not to get bored is knit.

MME. TÉPAN.   But tell me, do all the soldiers get bored the way you two do?

ZÉPO.   That depends on what they do for relaxation.

ZAPO.   Same thing over on our side.

M. TÉPAN.   Well then, let's stop the war.

ZÉPO.   But how?

M. TÉPAN.   Very easy. You tell your buddies that the enemy doesn't want to fight, and you tell the same thing to your comrades. And everybody goes home.

ZAPO.   Terrific!

MME. TÉPAN.   That way you can finish fixing the iron.

ZAPO.   How come nobody ever thought of that before?

MME. TÉPAN. It takes your father to come up with ideas like that. Don't forget he's a Normal School graduate, and a philatelist, too.

ZÉPO. But what will all the field-marshals and the corporals do?

M. TÉPAN. We'll give 'em guitars and castanets to keep 'em quiet.

ZÉPO. Excellent idea.

M. TÉPAN. See how easy it is? It's all settled.

ZÉPO. We'll wow 'em.

ZAPO. Boy, will my buddies be glad!

MME. TÉPAN. What do you say we celebrate and put on that paso-doble we were listening to before?

ZÉPO. Wonderful!

ZAPO. Yes, put on the record, Mama.

[MME. TÉPAN *puts on the record. She winds the phonograph and waits. Not a sound is heard.*]

M. TÉPAN. You can't hear anything.

MME. TÉPAN (*going to the phonograph*). Oh! . . . I made a boo-boo! Instead of putting on a record, I put on a beret.

[*She puts the record on. A lively pasodoble is heard.* ZAPO *dances with* ZÉPO; MME. TÉPAN *with her husband.*

The field telephone rings. None of the group hears it. They go on dancing in a lively manner.

The phone rings again. The dancing continues. Battle breaks out once more with a great din of bombs, rifle fire and the crackle of machine-guns. Having noticed nothing, the two couples keep on dancing gaily.

A sudden machine-gun blast mows them all down. They fall to the ground, stone dead. One bullet seems to have nicked the phonograph: the music keeps repeating the same strain over and over, like a record with a scratch in it. We hear this repeated strain for the remainder of the play.

From the left, the two CORPSMEN *enter, carrying the empty stretcher.*]

FAST CURTAIN

Questions

1.   In a play, we can often become involved in several attitudes or conflicting attitudes toward a subject. What are the attitudes of the characters in this play toward war? Which character, if any, represents the author's attitude?

2.   Why are Zapo and Zépo portrayed as alike or almost identical? Can you tell them apart? Why is Zapo afraid of Zépo?

3.   The picnic on the battlefield is absurd, of course, but does it make any sober comment about outdated and modern views of warfare? Or does it comment on the attitudes of those who do not fight and those who do?

4.   What is the significance of the incident involving the disappointed Red Cross corpsmen? Why is their disappointment ironic?

5.   No one in the play wants to kill. Why, then, are they involved in war? Why is it effective to keep off stage the generals, the machine gunners, the voice on the other end of the telephone, and others who do kill? Why are the parents and the two soldiers killed at the end?

6.   Why is the war in the play being fought?

Composition

1.   Write your own one-act play about war. Keep the setting simple and the characters few. Try to express your attitude without stating it explicitly. The play need not take place on a battlefield. Survey this book for ideas about settings and situations.

2.   Compare Arrabal's treatment of war with that of another playwright in a particular play. Consider, for example, Bertolt Brecht's *Mother Courage,* Jean Giraudoux's *A Tiger at the Gates,* or Shakespeare's *Henry IV, Part I* or *Henry V.* For a look of war from a civilian point of view, see Arthur Miller's *All My Sons* or Georg Kaiser's *The Raft of the Medusa.*

3.   A study of Arrabal's plays would make a good term paper topic. A selection of his works is handily collected in *Guernica and other plays* published by Grove Press. For more information on Arrabal, see Martin Esslin's *The Theatre of the Absurd.*

2. *Dulce et Decorum Est*

―――――――――――

WILFRED OWEN

Bent double, like old beggars under sacks,
Knock-kneed, coughing like hags, we cursed through sludge,
Till on the haunting flares we turned our backs,
And towards our distant rest began to trudge.
Men marched asleep. Many had lost their boots,
But limped on, blood-shod. All went lame, all blind;
Drunk with fatigue; deaf even to the hoots
Of gas-shells dropping softly behind.

Gas! GAS! Quick, boys! An ecstasy of fumbling,
Fitting the clumsy helmets just in time,
But someone still was yelling out and stumbling
And flound'ring like a man in fire or lime.—
Dim through the misty panes and thick green light,
As under a green sea, I saw him drowning.

In all my dreams before my helpless sight
He plunges at me, guttering, choking, drowning.

If in some smothering dreams, you too could pace
Behind the wagon that we flung him in,

And watch the white eyes writhing in his face,
His hanging face, like a devil's sick of sin,
If you could hear, at every jolt, the blood
Come gargling from the froth-corrupted lungs
Bitten as the cud
Of vile, incurable sores on innocent tongues,—
My friend, you would not tell with such high zest
To children ardent for some desperate glory,
The old Lie: *Dulce et decorum est*
Pro patria mori.

Questions

1.   The quotation in the last two lines and in the title is from Horace: "It is sweet and honorable to die for one's country." What concrete details does the narrator use to justify calling the quotation "the old Lie"?

2.   Because of the allusion in its title, this poem must be set against the notion of the classical hero-warrior who is always strong and upright in battle and who dies nobly and well. What images does Owen use to undercut this notion? Do you feel that the victim here should be dishonored for not dying well?

3.   Mist, the green sea, and dreams are often used in poetry to convey the sense of softness and unreality. How does Owen manipulate these concepts to make them horribly real?

Composition

1.   Is there a cause you would die for? Or is there a cause that you would have once, but would no longer die for? Write an essay that answers one of these questions and gives reasons for your stand.

3. *I Bombed the Barges*

THE PILOT OF A
BLENHEIM BOMBER

The narrator is a twenty-eight-year-old Scot who has raided nearly
all the invasion ports, from Flushing to Brest, on some night or
another since the first British onslaught began in early September.

If anything, Air Ministry bulletins have minimized the scale and
intensity of these R.A.F. attacks, which went on from twilight to
dawn without intermission until the last week of October. The im-
minence of the invasion threat probably inspired the sustained
ferocity of the raids. They have laid waste every port and harbor
from Holland to the Atlantic seaboard of France and smashed all
German hopes of a landing in Britain and an early conclusion to the
war. Air power—the battering ram of the Luftwaffe—brought the
German Army to the Channel ports; air power—the might of the
R.A.F.—stopped it there.

Since the British expected to find considerable fighter opposition
at these ports, Blenheim bombers were used in preference to heavy
night bombers like the Wellingtons, Whitleys, and Hampdens. The
R.A.F. has plenty of Blenheims, which are fighter-bombers and
which could more than make up in speed and maneuverability what
they might sacrifice in sheer load capacity.

As it happened, the R.A.F. found little fighter opposition. But according to the pilots, the ground defenses were hotter than anything encountered in their raids over German territory. It is believed that large numbers of mobile A.A. batteries were taken away from home defense in Germany and packed around the Channel ports. At any rate, pilots on "sorties" into Germany reported a much easier time while the bombing of the barges was proceeding. In addition, most of the A.A. guns and ammunition captured from the French, Belgians, and Dutch were packed into the restricted areas round these ports. And the Blenheim's special qualities of speed and "handling" came in useful in facing and breaking through such a hell-fire of ground defense.

The nickname given by bomber crews to the coastline of the invasion ports is "Blackpool Front." Blackpool, in Lancashire, is Britain's Coney Island, famous in prewar days for grandiose illuminations and firework spectacles.

The pilot who tells this story is a rather rangy young man with a droll sense of humor and speech full of telling metaphors. Before the war he was a constructional engineer employed in his father's firm, which has built, among other things, most of the cinemas for a big group in Britain.

He is a completely professional type and grimly deplores the exigencies of this war, which has brought him to "knocking things down when I would rather be building them up." But apparently he can do both equally well.

This is the Captain's story: It was three o'clock in the morning. An hour before, I was sleeping peacefully in my warm bed at the airdrome; now I was encased in noisy, vibrating metal walls, rumbling southeast under the stars over the dark, hidden fields and sleeping villages of England. At 9,000 feet I turned on my oxygen supply and instructed my rear gunner and the bomb-aimer to do likewise. It was freezing-cold and we've learned from experience that oxygen helps warm the blood.

We were heading for Ostend. As I watched the vague, greenish glimmer from the radium-painted instrument dials, I ran over in my mind all that we had been told at the "briefing" that evening. Again I visualized the photograph which our Intelligence Officer had shown us: the rows of 100-foot barges, ten in a line, ten rows deep, lying in each of the four harbor basins. From the height at which the picture was taken, they looked like matchsticks loosely bundled together.

I again pictured the three arms of the jetties separating the basins, three black lines jutting out toward the harbor entrance and probably packed with military stores and men. But it was the barges I was after, and I began to review our method of attack. I decided I would not bomb up the basins. If I was even a tiny bit out, my bombs might miss the water space and hit the jetties. No, I would bomb diagonally across all four basins. Then *some* of the stick of bombs would be certain to hit barges.

I thought of my chances of getting in for a low attack without being spotted. They were good, because I was the leading aircraft of my squadron. The others were following me at three-minute intervals and behind them were squadrons from two other stations. It was to be a proper "do." We were to put Ostend out of the invasion business for some time to come.

But since I would be the first visitor that night, I hoped that the usual "reception committee" would not be at work and that I would be able to throttle back well out to sea and glide in unobserved. I knew some of our boys had been busy already at Dunkirk and Calais, but I still hoped that the panic there would not have affected the German gunners at Ostend.

Reflecting about these matters, I began to get a little worried. It was pitch black outside, but I wondered whether even the faint glow from the instrument panels would affect our vision. I'm a stickler on this subject of darkness. I won't have any light at all inside my aircraft on a night raid. It's not that we might be spotted by enemy watchers but that I need about twenty minutes to get my full night vision and the slightest glint of light puts me off for another twenty minutes. And if we were to make a surprise attack, both the bomb-aimer and I would have to be at our best to pick up the target and the outline of the jetties on such a moonless night. And it would have to be done almost instantly after we crossed the enemy coastline. If we didn't pick it up and bomb at once, I would have to open up the motors again for another run on to the barges. Then the band would begin to play and low bombing would be out of the question.

Just then my navigator switched on his shrouded hand torch to scan the map on his table. He sits in front of me and the table is hidden from my view by my instrument panel, but a tiny reflected glow touched the side windows of the cabin. I told him urgently to hurry with his position check and douse the torch, and then kicked myself for being so brusque. He was a good bomb-aimer, quick, calm and accurate, and this was his last trip with me, as he was leaving the squadron to go on a pilot's course. A good bomb-aimer makes all the difference in getting your job done quickly and successfully and getting the hell out of it. I was fed up at losing him, so I chatted to him mildly for a while about various details.

We were over the sea now, heading for Ostend. I could tell that by the different sound of the motors, which always change their note over the sea. I did the last-minute jobs, setting the bomb fuses and pressing down the bomb-selection switches so the packets would all leave in a stick. It won't be long now, I thought, settling down in the seat.

I put her up in a long, slow climb to 15,000, at which height I would begin my glide in from about ten miles out. I warned my navigator to make a close check on our speed and course so that he could tell me the right moment to throttle back and start down.

Halfway across the Channel, I saw the glow of fires, the flash of bombs, bursting shells, and a great cascade of tracers, "flaming onions," and other muck coming up on my right along the French coast, where other British bombers were hitting hard. But to my left and straight ahead there was complete darkness. "Still good," I thought, and concentrated on my flying and the instruments. The navigator left his bench and squatted forward over the bomb sight. He began to check various readings with me over the phones. Just then my rear gunner, perched in his lonely cubbyhole amidships, called out "Fighter!" I listened anxiously through the crackle of the phones. Then the direction. "Red [port beam] below." Instantly I kicked the rudder over and climbed, so as to give the gunner a fair go at it. I leveled and waited. Then the gunner again: "He's out of range. But he's seen us. He's stalking us, sir."

There was nothing to do but go down again and turn widely off course, hoping to lose him. For it was no use attempting to argue with him. I had a job to do. Meanwhile I made rapid calculations. If I did not shake him off quickly, all my plans for a silent approach to the barges would be upset and the following aircraft from my squadron would be on top of me. I thumped the handle of my stick with impatience. We dived, swerved, swung around again, and hoped for the best. As luck would have it, my gunner soon announced that the fighter had gone. I got back on my course, giving full throttle to make up for lost time.

The whole of "Blackpool Front" was now in near view. It was an amazing spectacle. The Calais docks were on fire. So was the waterfront of Boulogne, and glares extended for miles. The whole French coast seemed to be a barrier of flame broken only by intense white flashes of exploding bombs and varicolored incendiary tracers soaring and circling skyward.

The rear gunner, who had hardly uttered a word throughout the entire trip, was shouting excitedly through the "intercom." "Gawd! Look at that—and that!" I grinned to myself as he went burbling on. He never talks as a rule, never complains or tries to open up a line of gossip, as many rear gunners do, afflicted by the loneliness and cold of their job. Throughout many a raid he has spoken to me only when he has had to answer routine questions. As he once put it to me with a grin, "Sometimes I sits and thinks, and sometimes I just sits."

We were getting near now. But not a peep, not a glimmer from the darkness ahead. I made some last-minute adjustments and called to the navigator, who called out "Now!"

I throttled back and put the nose down. Pressing my head against the windows, I strained and peered out to pick up the first glimpse of the Ostend harbor works. The navigator had gone forward to squat over his bomb sight in the nose. The semi-silence after the steady roar of the motors was almost startling. The air stream rushing past us rose in a high, steady, whistling scream as we plunged down. I thought of the waiting gun crews hidden there far ahead in the darkness, the massed soldiers on the quays and in the barges, unaware of our coming. I felt exultant, tremendous. I felt like singing above the vast avenging crescendo of my bomber driving through the sky.

And then I thought, "They'll hear us! They'll hear us!" The drone of the motors was cut, but the scream of the air stream was now deafening. The Blenheim was trembling as we touched the top speed of the dive. In that instant the navigator called, "Left, left!" As I obeyed instantly with rudder pressure, I saw the harbor too—a black outline on the darkness. It rushed nearer and upward. "Steady! Ri-i-ght! Steady!" chanted the bomb-aimer. We were over the harbor front. I fought the stick, flickering my gaze to ground and back to the quivering altimeter needle. Down to 500. There were the four jetty arms. We were dead on line. A searchlight shot up to the right of us, miles out and too late. I had an instant's thought of my bomb-aimer crouched forward with his hand on the lever of the "Mickey Mouse" [R.A.F. slang for bomb-release device], his eyes glued on those barge-filled basins sliding down between the drift wires on the bomb sight. Then came the great, surging kick on the stick as the bombs left the plane. A second later he was through to me on the phones and calmly announced, "Bombs gone."

My waiting hand threw open the throttle levers in a flash. The motors thundered out. Hauling back on the stick, kicking at the rudder, we went up in a great, banking climb. As we went, I stared down and out through the windows. There they were! One, two, three, four vast flashes as my bombs struck. In the light of the last one, just as lightning will suddenly paint a whole landscape, I saw the outline of the jetties in vivid relief. Between them the water boiled with thin black shapes. They were barges flung end up and fragments turning slowly over and over in the air.

Then came a most gigantic crash. We were nearly 2,000 feet up now and well away from the jetties, but the whole aircraft pitched over, as if a giant blow had struck us underneath. A vivid flash enveloped us and lingered, as sound burst round our ears. It was a blinding white flash like a great sheet of daylight stuck in between the dark. While all hell broke loose round us, I fought like mad to get control of the bomber. But all the time my mind was blankly wondering—half stunned as I was—what the devil had we hit. Afterward I learned that the last bomb had struck a group of mines stacked on a jetty waiting to be loaded aboard the mine-layers. Photographs taken the next morning showed two stone jetties blown away to the water's edge, all barges vanished from the inner basins, and devastation over a mile radius!

Then the searchlights got me. I plunged inland to dodge them, but they held, and the sky all round us was packed with every kind of muck arching over us and all around. It was a bad few minutes, and once or twice I thought we would never get out. In their mass of colored bursts the flak [German anti-aircraft fire] was crazily beautiful but horrible. The whole interior of my aircraft was lit up. I saw my navigator sitting up at my feet rubbing his head. He had been flung out of his compartment when we turned over in that great explosion.

There was a new kind of fiery flak which followed us and stuck close on either side. It resembled the three colored balls of a pawnbroker's sign. They frightened me. I watched them diving and climbing wildly, and dodged as best I could. They were probably clues to my position for their fighters, but they looked damnably dangerous. Somehow—I don't know how—we were out. I turned again and headed out to sea. Taking stock of ourselves, I called up the rear gunner. "I'm O.K.," he said, "but I didn't expect a ride in a rocket." My navigator said that he had been laid out when he was flung at my feet, but all he had now was a bad headache. Turning again along the coast, I saw more and more great flashes as others of my squadron went into Ostend. The whole sky was packed with A.A. bursts and I counted twenty great fires at different places round the harbor. Against the flames, the whole town stood out clearly. Most of the squadron, I reflected, would have had a free run in from the sea while the batteries were concentrating on me inland. In the din of that first great explosion their approaching engines would not have been heard. They couldn't have wished for a brighter target.

Then we swung around and headed for home. Behind us, yet another of the German Army's invasion ports was a bonfire on the skyline. The dawn was coming up across my right shoulder. England lay in her guarded sleep just ahead of us. The engines droned on. We were tired but somehow peaceful and happy as we quietly munched our rations.

Questions

1. The pilot of the bomber is described as a man who "grimly deplores the exigencies of war." Does his own account of the mission bear out this description?

2. Consider the effect of the bombing—the tremendous explosion that tumbles even the plane. How do you explain the pilot's feelings of peace and happiness that follow the destruction—and probably the death—he has caused?

3. What are some of the metaphors and similes the pilot uses? Are they effective in the context of war?

4. What makes the pilot's description of the bomb run (beginning "I throttled back and put the nose down. . . .") so effective?

Composition

1. Write about this incident from the point of view of the tail gunner or from the point of view of the enemy soldier who first hears the plane and sends up the probing searchlight "miles out and too late."

2. Using this essay and John Hersey's "Hiroshima: August 6, 1945" as your evidence, argue for or against aerial bombing in warfare.

3. Try to create the total sense of a bombing in a pictorial-verbal collage. Collect headlines and other phrases and words from newspapers and magazines. Gather photographs and other illustrations from the same sources. Certainly consider using material you have made yourself—drawings, photographs, poems, and the like. Finally select and arrange your material with paste and rubber cement on a large sheet of heavy paper or cardboard. Appeal mainly to the eye. Try to capture the paradoxical mixture of horror and beauty that is the inevitable quality of a holocaust.

4. Farraj

T. E. LAWRENCE

After Joyce and Dawnay had gone, I rode off from Aba el Lissan, with Mirzuk. Our starting day promised to crown the spring-freshness of this lofty tableland. A week before there had been a furious blizzard, and some of the whiteness of the snow seemed to have passed into the light. The ground was vivid with new grass; and the sunlight, which slanted across us, pale like straw, mellowed the fluttering wind.

With us journeyed two thousand Sirhan camels, carrying our ammunition and food. For the convoy's sake we marched easily, to reach the railway after dark. A few of us rode forward, to search the line by daylight, and be sure of peace during the hours these scattered numbers would consume in crossing.

My bodyguard was with me, and Mirzuk had his Ageyl, with two famous racing camels. The gaiety of the air and season caught them. Soon they were challenging to races, threatening one another, or skirmishing. My imperfect camel-riding (and my mood) forbade me to thrust among the lads, who swung more to the north, while I worked on, ridding my mind of the lees of camp-clamour and intrigue. The abstraction of the desert landscape cleansed me, and rendered my mind vacant with its superfluous greatness: a greatness achieved not by the addition of thought to its emptiness, but by its subtraction. In the weakness of earth's life was mirrored the strength of heaven, so vast, so beautiful, so strong.

Near sunset the line became visible, curving spaciously across the disclosed land, among low tufts of grass and bushes. Seeing everything was peaceful I pushed on, meaning to halt beyond and watch the others over. There was always a little thrill in touching the rails which were the target of so many of our efforts.

As I rode up the bank my camel's feet scrambled in the loose ballast, and out of the long shadow of a culvert to my left, where, no doubt, he had slept all day, rose a Turkish soldier. He glanced wildly at me and at the pistol in my hand, and then with sadness at his rifle against the abutment, yards beyond. He was a young man; stout, but sulky-looking. I stared at him, and said, softly, "God is merciful." He knew the sound and sense of the Arabic phrase, and raised his eyes like a flash to mine, while his heavy sleep-ridden face began slowly to change into incredulous joy.

However, he said not a word. I pressed my camel's hairy shoulder with my foot, she picked her delicate stride across the metals and down the further slope, and the little Turk was man enough not to shoot me in the back, as I rode away, feeling warm towards him, as ever towards a life one has saved. At a safe distance I glanced back. He put thumb to nose, and twinkled his fingers at me.

We lit a coffee-fire as beacon for the rest, and waited till their dark lines passed by. Next day we marched to Wadi el Jinz; to flood-pools, shallow eyes of water set in wrinkles of the clay, their rims lashed about with scrubby stems of brushwood. The water was grey, like the marly valley bed, but sweet. There we rested for the night, since the Zaagi had shot a bustard, and Xenophon did rightly call its white meat good. While we feasted the camels feasted. By the bounty of spring they were knee-deep in succulent green-stuff.

A fourth easy march took us to the Atara, our goal, where our allies, Mifleh, Fahad and Adhub, were camped. Fahad was still stricken, but Mifleh, with honeyed words, came out to welcome us, his face eaten up by greed, and his voice wheezy with it.

Our plan, thanks to Allenby's lion-share, promised simply. We would, when ready, cross the line to Themed, the main Beni Sakhr watering. Thence under cover of a screen of their cavalry we would move in Madeba, and fit it as our headquarters, while Allenby put the Jericho-Salt road in condition. We ought to link up with the British comfortably without firing a shot.

Meanwhile we had only to wait in the Atatir, which to our joy were really green, with every hollow a standing pool, and the valley beds of tall grass prinked with flowers. The chalky ridges, sterile with salt, framed the water-channel delightfully. From their tallest point we could look north and south, and see how the rain, running down, had painted the valleys across the white in broad stripes of green, sharp and firm like brush-strokes. Everything was growing, and daily the picture was fuller and brighter till the desert became like a rank water-meadow. Playful packs of winds came crossing and tumbling over one another, their wide, brief gusts surging through the grass, to lay it momentarily in swathes of dark and light satin, like young corn after the roller. On the hill we sat and shivered before these sweeping shadows, expecting a heavy blast— and there would come into our faces a warm and perfumed breath, very gentle, which passed away behind us as a silver-grey light down the plain of green. Our fastidious camels grazed an hour or so, and then lay down to digest, bringing up stomach-load after stomach-load of butter-smelling green cud, and chewing weightily.

At last news came that the English had taken Amman. In half an hour we were making for Themed, across the deserted line. Later messages told us that the English were falling back, and though we had forewarned the Arabs of it, yet they were troubled. A further messenger reported how the English had just fled from Salt. This was plainly contrary to Allenby's intention, and I swore straight out that it was not true. A man galloped in to say that the English had broken only a few rails south of Amman, after two days of vain assaults against the town. I grew seriously disturbed in the conflict of rumour, and sent Adhub, who might be trusted not to lose his head, to Salt with a letter for Chetwode or Shea, asking for a note on the real situation. For the intervening hours we tramped restlessly over the fields of young barley, our minds working out plan after plan with feverish activity.

Very late at night Adhub's racing horse-hooves echoed across the valley and he came in to tell us that Jemal Pasha was now in Salt, victorious, hanging those local Arabs who had welcomed the English. The Turks were still chasing Allenby far down the Jordan Valley. It was thought that Jerusalem would be recovered. I knew enough of my countrymen to reject that possibility; but clearly things were very wrong. We slipped off, bemused, to the Atatir again.

This reverse, being unawares, hurt me the more. Allenby's plan had seemed modest, and that we should so fall down before the Arabs was deplorable. They had never trusted us to do the great things which I foretold; and now their independent thoughts set out to enjoy the springtide here. They were abetted by some gipsy families from the north with the materials of their tinkering trade on donkeys. The Zebn tribesmen greeted them with a humour I little understood—till I saw that, beside their legitimate profits of handicraft, the women were open to other advances.

Particularly they were easy to the Ageyl; and for a while they prospered exceedingly, since our men were eager and very generous. I also made use of them. It seemed a pity to be at a loose end so near to Amman, and not bother to look at it. So Farraj and I hired three of the merry little women, wrapped ourselves up like them, and strolled through the village. The visit was successful, though my final determination was that the place should be left alone. We had one evil moment, by the bridge, when we were returning. Some Turkish soldiers crossed our party, and taking us all five for what we looked, grew much too friendly. We showed a coyness, and good turn of speed for gipsy women, and escaped intact. For the future I decided to resume my habit of wearing ordinary British soldiers' rig in enemy camps. It was too brazen to be suspect.

After this I determined to order the Indians from Azrak back to Feisal, and to return myself. We started on one of those clean dawns which woke up the senses with the sun, while the intellect, tired after the thinking of the night, was yet abed. For an hour or two on such a morning the sounds, scents and colours of the world struck man individually and directly, not filtered through or made typical by thought; they seemed to exist sufficiently by themselves, and the lack of design and of carefulness in creation no longer irritated.

We marched southward along the railway, expecting to cross the slower-moving Indians from Azrak; our little party on prize camels swooping from one point of vantage to another, on the look-out. The still day encouraged us to speed over all the flint-strewn ridges, ignoring the multitude of desert paths which led only to the abandoned camps of last year, or of the last thousand or ten thousand years: for a road, once trodden into such flint and limestone, marked the face of the desert for so long as the desert lasted.

By Faraifra we saw a little patrol of eight Turks marching up the line. My men, fresh after the holiday in the Atatir, begged me to ride on them. I thought it too trifling, but when they chafed, agreed. The younger ones instantly rushed forward at a gallop. I ordered the rest across the line, to drive the enemy away from their shelter behind a culvert. The Zaagi, a hundred yards to my right, seeing what was wanted, swerved aside at once. Mohsin followed him a moment later, with his section; whilst Abdulla and I pushed forward steadily on our side, to take the enemy on both flanks together.

Farraj, riding in front of everyone, would not listen to our cries nor notice the warning shots fired past his head. He looked round at our manœuvre, but himself continued to canter madly towards the bridge, which he reached before the Zaagi and his party had crossed the line. The Turks held their fire, and we supposed them gone down the further side of the embankment into safety; but as Farraj drew rein beneath the archway, there was a shot, and he seemed to fall or leap out of the saddle, and disappeared. A while after, the Zaagi got into position on the bank and his party fired twenty or thirty ragged shots, as though the enemy was still there.

I was very anxious about Farraj. His camel stood unharmed by the bridge, alone. He might be hit, or might be following the enemy. I could not believe that he had deliberately ridden up to them in the open and halted; yet it looked like it. I sent Feheyd to the Zaagi and told him to rush along the far side as soon as possible, whilst we went at a fast trot straight in to the bridge.

We reached it together, and found there one dead Turk, and Farraj terribly wounded through the body, lying by the arch just as he had fallen from his camel. He looked unconscious; but, when we dismounted, greeted us, and then fell silent, sunken in that loneliness which came to hurt men who believed death near. We tore his clothes away and looked uselessly at the wound. The bullet had smashed right through him, and his spine seemed injured. The Arabs said at once that he had only a few hours to live.

We tried to move him, for he was helpless, though he showed no pain. We tried to stop the wide, slow bleeding, which made poppy-splashes in the grass; but it seemed impossible, and after a while he told us to let him alone, as he was dying, and happy to die, since he had no care of life. Indeed, for long he had been so, and men very tired and sorry often fell in love with death, with that triumphal weakness coming home after strength has been vanquished in a last battle.

While we fussed about him Abd el Latif shouted an alarm. He could see about fifty Turks working up the line towards us, and soon after a motor trolley was heard coming from the north. We were only sixteen men, and had an impossible position. I said we must retire at once, carrying Farraj with us. They tried to lift him, first in his cloak, afterwards in a blanket; but consciousness was coming back, and he screamed so pitifully that we had not the heart to hurt him more.

We could not leave him where he was, to the Turks, because we had seen them burn alive our hapless wounded. For this reason we were all agreed, before action, to finish off one another, if badly hurt: but I had never realized that it might fall to me to kill Farraj.

I knelt down beside him, holding my pistol near the ground by his head, so that he should not see my purpose; but he must have guessed it, for he opened his eyes, and clutched me with his harsh, scaly hand, the tiny hand of these unripe Nejd fellows. I waited a moment, and he said, "Daud will be angry with you," the old smile coming back so strangely to this grey shrinking face. I replied, "salute him from me." He returned the formal answer, "God will give you peace," and at last wearily closed his eyes.

The Turkish trolley was now very close, swaying down the line towards us like a dung-beetle: and its machine-gun bullets stung the air about our heads as we fled back into the ridges. Mohsin led Farraj's camel, on which were his sheepskin and trappings, still with the shape of his body in them, just as he had fallen by the bridge. Near dark we halted; and the Zaagi came whispering to me that all were wrangling as to who should ride the splendid animal next day. He wanted her for himself; but I was bitter that these perfected dead had again robbed my poverty: and to cheapen the great loss with a little one I shot the poor beast with my second bullet.

Then the sun set on us. Through the breathless noon in the valleys of Kerak the prisoned air had brooded stagnantly without relief, while the heat sucked the perfume from the flowers. With darkness the world moved once more, and a breath from the west crept out over the desert. We were miles from the grass and flowers, but suddenly we felt them all about us, as waves of this scented air drew past us with a sticky sweetness. However, quickly it faded, and the night-wind, damp and wholesome, followed. Abdulla brought me supper, rice and camel-meat (Farraj's camel). Afterwards we slept.

The Polish Rider by Rembrandt copyright The Frick Collection, New York

The subject of this painting is not known, and its armed rider has long posed a mystery to those who have viewed this work. Look carefully at this painting—at the details, the lighting, and the placement of objects. Pose three questions about it for the class to discuss. How would you answer your own questions?

Questions

1.   In this chapter from *The Seven Pillars of Wisdom,* Lawrence tries to give order and meaning to his personal experience of war. Can you infer here his attitudes toward war?

2.   Lawrence gives much attention to the natural background against which the action takes place. He describes it; he comments on it. What does the setting contribute to the meaning of his experience? Is the last paragraph of the selection an appropriate and effective conclusion to this chapter?

3.   Twice Lawrence is faced with killing a man. How do the two incidents relate to each other? Why does Lawrence let his enemy go?

4.   Was Farraj's death useless?

Composition

1.   Using the basic details provided by Lawrence, write about the death of Farraj from another point of view. You might try writing from the point of view of the Zaagi. If so, would you include the incident concerning Farraj's camel? Write about Farraj's death from the point of view of an enemy observer, or from Farraj's own point of view.

5. My First Experience of Fighting—Alamein

KEITH DOUGLAS

As we passed behind the Grant, labouring in second gear, a 50-mm. shot came through the side of our turret with an immense clang. The tank stopped and rolled back a few yards. My first sensation was that the whole turret had collapsed inwards on us and was pinning us in. I couldn't open my eyes, the right side of my face seemed to be very sore, and there was a small pain in my left leg. I heard the Corporal say: "Get out, sir, we've been hit" as though from a long way off, and simultaneously I was able to move, as if his voice had broken a spell. I climbed out on to the back of the tank, with the earphones still on and the microphone dangling on my chest. I was able to open my eyes for a second but they closed themselves and tears poured out from under the lids. I realized the wireless was still working, and said: "King Five, my horse has copped it. Wireless O.K., but we shan't be able to take any further part in the show. I'll just have a look at the damage and tell you the extent." "King Five, that's the second time. You *must not* say such things over the air," said Picca-dilly Jim. I could not see what harm it could do if I had said clearly, "My tank has been hit," since the enemy must have observed the hit, but supposing my reasoning must not be working properly, said:

Alamein to Zem Zem by Keith Douglas; © Marie Douglas, 1966; Published by Chilmark Press.

"King Five, sorry. I'm a bit dizzy. Over," and Piccadilly Jim replied, characteristically: "King Five, I'm sorry you're dizzy. But you really must not say these things. Now take care of yourself. Off."

I now had my eyes open and could see that the Grant beside us was burning beautifully. It must have been hit a few seconds after us. The faces of its crew and of my own corporal watched me from a German vehicle pit a few yards away. I climbed off the tank and with the idea of saving my kit from the risk of catching fire, hauled my valise and pack into the pit. I said to the Corporal: "Where's the driver?" "He must be in there still, sir." I went and peered in at the driver's window in the front of the Crusader, which was not closed down. Inside, Dunn the driver, lay with his eyes closed, his face chalky and his mouth open, showing a few yellow teeth and a lolling tongue. Like Old Man Mose, he didn't make a single move and I thought he was dead, but as I was turning away his eyes opened and he said almost in a whisper, "My neck, my neck." I called two of the others out of the pit and we were able to get him out, although I'm afraid we hurt him a lot doing it. We lowered him into the pit, where he complained of intolerable pain. I remembered that the officers had all been given individual morphia syringes, containing one dose, before the battle, and searched my pockets vainly for mine. I looked round and saw that Black was still where he had stopped when we were hit, some ten yards from the blazing Grant, and gazing vacantly at the edge of the bowl about ten yards in front of him. I thought, doesn't the bloody fool know it'll blow up in a minute, and went across to him. He did not see me. I stood beside his tank and shouted at him, but he had his earphones on, and continued to stare stolidly ahead, like a cow. "Give me your morphia," I shouted. The Grant beside us blew up with a great roar, twelve yards away. The twenty-four tons of metal disintegrated; the turret flying one way, the sides and suspension wheels another, left a mass of burning wreckage, and one of the great rubber tracks uncoiled like a dead snake. By some chance I was hit by someone's bedding and found myself hurled against the side of the Crusader, wrapped from head to foot in blankets. I glared up at Black like a Red Indian, and he stared down at me with a wondering eye. He was evidently trying to decide why I was dressed in blankets. I shouted again, "Give me your *morphia syringe*." He took off his earphones and after shouting only once more, I saw him fumbling inside the turret. He handed it out to me. "Now go away before you're hit," I said. I went back to the pit.

The Corporal injected the morphia into Dunn's arm: the needle was very blunt and a good deal of the stuff flowed out of a crack at the base of the needle and dribbled on the skin. Dunn did not seem any better for the injection. This was not surprising since it later turned out that we had been given by mistake a preparation for waking up people under anaesthetic.

The shells continued falling, and no one was much inclined to stir out of the pit. But the engine of my Crusader was still running: the shot had made a clean round hole in the underside of the turret, and must have passed within a few inches of my stomach and smashed against the base of the six-pounder. I had had a look at the damage during the business of getting Dunn out, and now that he was as settled as possible I felt I ought to move the tank out of the area of shell fire. When I stood up to go and do this the Corporal said there were half a dozen packets of Players on top of the wireless set, and would I please bring them back with me. I got the Players first and then climbed out of the top of the tank and in again through the front. I settled myself in the driver's compartment, revved the engine, and engaged first gear. I let up the clutch as slowly as possible and the tank began to grind forward. When I had gathered speed I engaged second gear but the engine sputtered, coughed, and stalled. I tried to restart it in vain. So I pulled myself up and out again, dropping off the bows of the tank on to the ground. The shell-fire seemed to have slackened in our neighbourhood and I looked round the area. On the edge of the bowl, about fifty yards away, was a German tank.

It must have arrived after I had stopped moving, for the commander of it was gazing over my head at the ridges far behind me. I dodged down and looked hastily round. Until this moment I had felt comforted by the presence all round our pit of the "C" Squadron Shermans. In the back of my mind I had supposed someone would soon arrive to pick us out of our hole. My last glimpse of the enemy had been of a tank escaping hurriedly westwards, and I had had no doubt in my mind that the nearest Germans were a mile or two across the valley. For one tank to advance again against a squadron would be madness. But I saw now that although all the Shermans were still there, those reassuring shapes which I had seen out of the corner of my eye while I was extricating Dunn, injecting morphia, bandaging —there was not a living man in any of them. They were dead tanks, burning, smouldering or silent and useless. This was the biggest shock.

"Capture," I thought suddenly. "I shall be captured." There was no sign of the regiment. Only the shells of tanks, and the enemy, coolly surveying the landscape. If I ran to the hole they would find us all. I think I was as near panic as I have ever been. My thoughts flickered with my glance over all possible refuges. I began to run, keeping my tank between me and the enemy: I was bound to come into the open and to make an easy mark for their machine-gun, and I thought of this and accepted the thought. I did not care if they shot me but I was unnerved by the thought of capture. I ran about two hundred yards. After that the headache of the early morning reasserted itself, the sore in my leg throbbed insistently under its dirty bandages, the scorched places on my face and the scratches on my leg made themselves felt, and I had no more breath to run; I was quite exhausted. I began walking, too tired to care any more even about escape, until I should have a breathing space.

I walked forward blindly and almost tripped over a man on the ground. He was a "C" Squadron corporal, and his right foot was not there: the leg ended in a sort of tattered brush of bone and flesh. He said something which I could not hear, or which my mind would not grasp. After he had said it twice, I realized he was asking me not to leave him behind. To carry him seemed to my tired muscles and lungs impossible. I looked ahead and saw the sandhills stretching for an eternity, without a sign of life. "Kneel down," he said. "I can get on your back." I got on my knees and he fastened a grip on me like the old man of the sea. I tried to stand up, and at last achieved it, swaying and sweating, with the man on my back; his good leg and his stump tucked under my arms, his hands locked at my throat.

"Don't grip my throat so hard if you can help it," I said. He relaxed his hold at once and slid his hands down to my chest. I began to walk forward, with little idea of what I was going to do. As far as I could see I had half to three-quarters of a mile to go under the eye of the German tank commander, before I could cross a ridge and get out of his sight. No shot was fired, while I walked about fifty yards. Then an officer and two men of "C" Squadron came out of a square pit where they were sheltering and helped me in with my burden, which we lowered carefully. Bill, the officer had not long rejoined the regiment from a special job. He and the others began to put a shell dressing on the wounded man's leg, while I sat panting and regaining my breath. I realized I was still clutching two or three packets of Players which I had taken from my tank, so I handed them round. I told Bill about the German tank: I was still obsessed with the idea of escaping capture. I think if it had been hailing machine-gun bullets I would have stepped out into them without caring. My mind was not working properly. "If we all stay here," I said to Bill, "we shall probably be captured. I think someone ought to go back and try to get a vehicle to get us out." This was quite a sensible suggestion, but a wish was father to it. Bill agreed and said: "You go. These are my chaps, so I'll stay. Corporal Hicks, Dumeny, Cairns, you go back." We stood up and left the pit. A machine-gun somewhere opened up; I heard the noise of it, but did not see any sign that the shots were aimed at us. The men with me were walking along bent double as though searching the ground. I said to them: "It's no good ducking down. If you're going to be hit you'll be hit. Run across the open ground. Run." They began to trot reluctantly, and I ran ahead. Presently I saw two men crawling on the ground, wriggling forward very slowly in a kind of embrace.

As I came up to them I recognized one of them as Robin, the R.H.A. Observation Officer whose aid I had been asking earlier in the day: I recognized first his fleece-lined suede waistcoat and polished brass shoulder titles and then his face, strained and tired with pain. His left foot was smashed to pulp, mingled with the remainder of a boot. But as I spoke to Robin saying, "Have you got a tourniquet, Robin?" and he answered apologetically: "I'm afraid I haven't, Peter," I looked at the second man. Only his clothes distinguished him as a human being, and they were badly charred. His face had gone: in place of it was a huge yellow vegetable. The eyes blinked in it, eyes without lashes, and a grotesque huge mouth dribbled and moaned like a child exhausted with crying.

Robin's mangled leg was not bleeding: a paste of blood and sand, or congealed slabs of blood, covered it. I thought it would be better left as it was than bandaged, now that the air had closed it. "I'll go on back," I said, "and get hold of something to pick you up, a scout car or something. Stay here." I ran on. Before I had gone a hundred yards I was ashamed: my own mind accused me of running to escape, rather than running for help. But I hurried on, determined to silence these accusations by getting a vehicle of some kind and bringing it back, in the face of the enemy if necessary. I knew that if only I could gain the cover of the ridge and stop to think, and if I could find where the regiment had gone, I should be able to reorganize myself and go back, as I had after the first encounter with the tank.

Round a ridge of sand beside me the new lieutenant came walking. He raised a hand in salute and began to talk in a foolish flow of words about how his tank had been hit in the engine and why it had happened and how it would never have happened if only he had done such and such a thing, *und so weiter*. I walked beside him. I said: "We must find the chaps, and get something to get the people out of those holes, and tell Piccadilly Jim how close the enemy are." I was searching the ground ahead with my eyes, my companion looking at the ground by his feet. We almost walked past the remains of the regiment, drawn up on our left behind a ridge, because I was looking for them ahead and he was not looking at all. The nearest vehicle was Mousky's scout car, which I had had in mind, and I ran across towards it. In it sat Mousky and his driver. Another infantryman stood beside it. As we came closer I could see it was buried over its differential in sand, and would take anything up to an hour to shift. No one had yet begun to try. But beyond it was the scout car belonging to the Technical adjutant, Bert Pyeman, an ex-regular N.C.O., contemporary of Mac's. Bert was driving away from me. I shouted at him, but two of the Shermans fired simultaneously and my voice was drowned. Before I could shout again, my companion said: "Look out. There's a trip wire." I knew already; I had just tripped it. I should have thrown myself down at once, but a sort of resignation prevented me, and I walked on a few steps before the mine exploded.

I remained standing, numbed. It seemed impossible that anything could hit so hard and leave me on my feet: and as feeling came back, I shrank from movement. But the explosion of a second mine suggested to me that I ought to throw myself down, and I toppled forward and sprawled on the sand. A third mine went off, further away. I was aware of the new subaltern lying on the other side of the trip wire, which stretched between us as taut as ever. It was a bright new wire strung through wooden pegs: I realized that I had seen it and discounted it because of its newness, and because subconsciously I had come to expect such things to be cunningly hidden. People ran towards us from Mousky's scout car. I shouted to them: "Look out for mines. Don't explode any more." One of them said mistakenly as he came up, "*You're* all right, sir," in a soothing sort of voice. I found I could raise one arm and waved it at Bert Pyeman whose attention the bang had attracted. He swung his little beetle of a car round and came across to us. "Don't try to get up, Peter," he said. I couldn't even try now: and it seemed incredible that a minute or two ago I had shouted out, for now I could only raise a whisper, in which I said: "Can you get me out of here?" somewhat unnecessarily. "O.K. old boy, we'll get you out. Can you heave yourself on to the back of the Dingo if we support you?" Bert had finished putting a very tight bandage on my right foot, which had been bleeding a lot. "Yes, I think so," I said.

Questions

1.   The central figure in this narrative is a British tank commander in battle for the first time. How would you describe his response to warfare?

2.   Alamein is usually considered to be one of the great battles in history, a battle that produced many heroes. Are there any actions in this narrative that might be called heroic? How are they treated by the narrator?

3.   Do you accept the narrator's explanation for his failure to heed the mine-trip wire? Is his explanation in any way a comment on war?

Composition

1.   The Battle of Alamein is worth some research. A fruitful approach would be to survey the copious literature on the battle and to write a paper called "The Reality of Alamein." What was the reality of that battle? Consider the accounts of Field Marshal Bernard Montgomery in his *Memoirs* and of Field Marshal Irwin Rommel in *The Rommel Papers,* edited by B. H. Liddell-Hart. C. E. Lucas Phillips gives an historian's response in his *Alamein.*

2.   Douglas' narrative points up the confusion and absurdity of war. Humor and terror are often present in a single moment as in the narrator's encounter with a German tank. Make a collage that conveys the dual sense of terror and fun, of brutality and tenderness in war. Refer to composition problem 3 on page 30 for directions about a way to proceed with your collage.

6. *Vergissmeinicht*

KEITH DOUGLAS

Three weeks gone and the combatants gone,
returning over the nightmare ground
we found the place again, and found
the soldier sprawling in the sun.

The frowning barrel of his gun
overshadowing. As we came on
that day, he hit my tank with one
like the entry of a demon.

Look. Here in the gunpit spoil
the dishonoured picture of his girl
who has put: *Steffi. Vergissmeinicht*
in a copybook gothic script.

We see him almost with content
abased, and seeming to have paid
and mocked at by his own equipment
that's hard and good when he's decayed.

But she would weep to see today
how on his skin the swart flies move;

Collected Poems by Keith Douglas; © by Marie Douglas, 1966; published by Chilmark Press.

the dust upon the paper eye
and the burst stomach like a cave.

For here the lover and killer are mingled
who had one body and one heart.
And death who had the soldier singled
has done the lover mortal hurt.

Questions

1. What meanings can you find in the image of the dead soldier's equipment which seems to mock him?

2. In the view of the narrator, the German soldier is a lover and a killer. Is recognition of this dual identity a new discovery for the narrator? Has he ever seen his victim in another way?

3. What is the effect of calling the girl's picture "dishonoured"? "*Vergissmeinicht*" means "forget me not." Why is the girl's inscription especially poignant in this situation?

4. In pausing by the body of the dead soldier, the narrator is showing his sympathy for the man and for the girl who will miss him. If the narrator could relive the moment of his first meeting with the soldier, do you believe that he would have wanted another outcome?

Composition

1. One can call this poem a retrospective work. The speaker returns in a moment of quiet to a scene where only a short time ago he had felt great pressure and urgency. Write about a personal experience in which you followed the same pattern. In your second look what meaning did you perceive that was not apparent the first time?

7. *The Man He Killed*

THOMAS HARDY

"HAD he and I but met
By some old ancient inn,
We should have sat us down to wet
Right many a nipperkin!

"But ranged as infantry,
And staring face to face,
I shot at him as he at me,
And killed him in his place.

"I shot him dead because—
Because he was my foe,
Just so: my foe of course he was;
That's clear enough; although

"He thought he'd 'list, perhaps,
Off-hand like—just as I—
Was out of work—had sold his traps—
No other reason why.

"Yes; quaint and curious war is!
You shoot a fellow down
You'd treat if met where any bar is,
Or help to half-a-crown."

Questions

1. How good is the reason the narrator gives for shooting the man?

2. Are "quaint" and "curious" good adjectives to use in describing war in this poem? What effect do these words have?

3. In the fourth stanza, the narrator sees likeness between himself and his foe. Is there in this likeness an implicit statement about the causes of war?

4. How would you describe the tone of this poem? Is it bitter? Angry? Resigned? Something else? What word choices does Hardy make to create the tone?

Composition

1. Organize and produce on audio tape a poetry reading like those you have doubtless heard at your school. Make war poetry your subject, and unify your readings with a commentary on the points of view expressed in the poems.

8. War in the Trenches

ERICH MARIA REMARQUE

. . .

The front is a cage in which we must await fearfully whatever may happen. We lie under the network of arching shells and live in a suspense of uncertainty. Over us Chance hovers. If a shot comes, we can duck, that is all; we neither know nor can determine where it will fall.

It is this Chance that makes us indifferent. A few months ago I was sitting in a dug-out playing skat; after a while I stood up and went to visit some friends in another dug-out. On my return nothing more was to be seen of the first one, it had been blown to pieces by a direct hit. I went back to the second and arrived just in time to lend a hand digging it out. In the interval it had been buried.

It is just as much a matter of chance that I am still alive as that I might have been hit. In a bomb-proof dug-out I may be smashed to atoms and in the open may survive ten hours' bombardment unscathed. No soldier outlives a thousand chances. But every soldier believes in Chance and trusts his luck.

．　．　．

We must look out for our bread. The rats have become much more numerous lately because the trenches are no longer in good condition. Detering says it is a sure sign of a coming bombardment.

The rats here are particularly repulsive, they are so fat—the kind we call corpse-rats. They have shocking, evil, naked faces, and it is nauseating to see their long, nude tails.

They seem to be mighty hungry. Almost every man has had his bread gnawed. Kropp wrapped his in his waterproof sheet and put it under his head, but he cannot sleep because they run over his face to get at it. Detering meant to outwit them: he fastened a thin wire to the roof and suspended his bread from it. During the night when he switched on his pocket-torch he saw the wire swinging to and fro. On the bread was riding a fat rat.

At last we put a stop to it. We cannot afford to throw the bread away, because already we have practically nothing left to eat in the morning, so we carefully cut off the bits of bread that the animals have gnawed.

The slices we cut off are heaped together in the middle of the floor. Each man takes out his spade and lies down prepared to strike. Detering, Kropp, and Kat hold their pocket-lamps ready.

After a few minutes we hear the first shuffling and tugging. It grows, now it is the sound of many little feet. Then the torches switch on and every man strikes at the heap, which scatters with a rush. The result is good. We toss the bits of rat over the parapet and again lie in wait.

Several times we repeat the process. At last the beasts get wise to it, or perhaps they have scented the blood. They return no more. Nevertheless, before morning the remainder of the bread on the floor has been carried off.

In the adjoining sector they attacked two large cats and a dog, bit them to death and devoured them.

Next day there is an issue of Edamer cheese. Each man gets almost a quarter of a cheese. In one way that is all to the good, for Edamer is tasty—but in another way it is vile, because the fat red balls have long been a sign of a bad time coming. Our forebodings increase as rum is served out. We drink it of course; but are not greatly comforted.

For days we loaf about and make war on the rats. Ammunition and hand-grenades become more plentiful. We even overhaul the bayonets—that is to say, the ones that have a saw on the blunt edge. If the fellows over there catch a man with one of those he's killed at sight. In the next sector some of our men were found whose noses were cut off and their eyes poked out with their own saw-bayonets. Their mouths and noses were stuffed with sawdust so that they suffocated.

Some of the recruits have bayonets of this kind; we take them away and give them the ordinary kind.

But the bayonet has practically lost its importance. It is usually the fashion now to charge with bombs and spades only. The sharpened spade is a more handy and many-sided weapon; not only can it be used for jabbing a man under the chin, but it is much better for striking with because of its greater weight; and if one hits between the neck and shoulder it easily cleaves as far down as the chest. The bayonet frequently jams on the thrust and then a man has to kick hard on the other fellow's belly to pull it out again; and in the interval he may easily get one himself. And what's more, the blade often gets broken off.

At night they send over gas. We expect the attack to follow and lie with our masks on, ready to tear them off as soon as the first shadow appears.

Dawn approaches without anything happening—only the everlasting, nerve-wracking roll behind the enemy lines, trains, trains, lorries, lorries; but what are they concentrating? Our artillery fires on it continually, but still it does not cease.

We have tired faces and avoid each other's eyes. "It will be like the Somme," says Kat gloomily. "There we were shelled steadily for seven days and nights." Kat has lost all his fun since we have been here, which is bad, for Kat is an old front-hog, and can smell what is coming. Only Tjaden seems pleased with the good rations and the rum; he thinks we might even go back to rest without anything happening at all.

It almost looks like it. Day after day passes. At night I squat in the listening-post. Above me the rockets and parachute-lights shoot up and float down again. I am cautious and tense, my heart thumps. My eyes turn again and again to the luminous dial of my watch; the hands will not budge. Sleep hangs on my eyelids, I work my toes in

my boots in order to keep awake. Nothing happens till I am re-
lieved;—only the everlasting rolling over there. Gradually we grow
calmer and play skat and poker continually. Perhaps we will be
lucky.

All day the sky is hung with observation balloons. There is a
rumour that the enemy are going to put tanks over and use low-flying
planes for the attack. But that interests us less than what we hear
of the new flame-throwers.

• • •

We wake up in the middle of the night. The earth booms.
Heavy fire is falling on us. We crouch into corners. We distinguish
shells of every calibre.

Each man lays hold of his things and looks again every minute
to reassure himself that they are still there. The dug-out heaves, the
night roars and flashes. We look at each other in the momentary
flashes of light, and with pale faces and pressed lips shake our
heads.

Every man is aware of the heavy shells tearing down the parapet, rooting up the embankment and demolishing the upper layers
of concrete. When a shell lands in the trench we note how the hollow, furious blast is like a blow from the paw of a raging beast of
prey. Already by morning a few of the recruits are green and vomit-
ing. They are too inexperienced.

Slowly the grey light trickles into the post and pales the flashes
of the shells. Morning is come. The explosion of mines mingles with
the gun-fire. That is the most dementing convulsion of all. The
whole region where they go up becomes one grave.

The reliefs go out, the observers stagger in, covered with dirt,
and trembling. One lies down in silence in the corner and eats, the
other, a reservist-reinforcement, sobs; twice he has been flung over
the parapet by the blast of the explosions without getting any more
than shell-shock.

The recruits are eyeing him. We must watch them, these things
are catching, already some lips begin to quiver. It is good that it is
growing daylight; perhaps the attack will come before noon.

The bombardment does not diminish. It is falling in the rear too.
As far as one can see it spouts fountains of mud and iron. A wide
belt is being raked.

The attack does not come, but the bombardment continues.

Slowly we become mute. Hardly a man speaks. We cannot make ourselves understood.

Our trench is almost gone. At many places it is only eighteen inches high, it is broken by holes, and craters, and mountains of earth. A shell lands square in front of our post. At once it is dark. We are buried and must dig ourselves out. After an hour the entrance is clear again, and we are calmer because we have had something to do.

• • •

Night again. We are deadened by the strain—a deadly tension that scrapes along one's spine like a gapped knife. Our legs refuse to move, our hands tremble, our bodies are a thin skin stretched painfully over repressed madness, over an almost irresistible, bursting roar. We have neither flesh nor muscles any longer, we dare not look at one another for fear of some incalculable thing. So we shut our teeth—it will end—it will end—perhaps we will come through.

Suddenly the nearer explosions cease. The shelling continues but it has lifted and falls behind us, our trench is free. We seize the hand-grenades, pitch them out in front of the dug-out and jump after them. The bombardment has stopped and a heavy barrage now falls behind us. The attack has come.

No one would believe that in this howling waste there could still be men; but steel helmets now appear on all sides out of the trench, and fifty yards from us a machine-gun is already in position and barking.

The wire-entanglements are torn to pieces. Yet they offer some obstacle. We see the storm-troops coming. Our artillery opens fire. Machine-guns rattle, rifles crack. The charge works its way across. Haie and Kropp begin with the hand-grenades. They throw as fast as they can, others pass them, the handles with the strings already pulled. Haie throws seventy-five yards, Kropp sixty, it has been measured, the distance is important. The enemy as they run cannot do much before they are within forty yards.

We recognize the distorted faces, the smooth helmets: they are French. They have already suffered heavily when they reach the remnants of the barbed-wire entanglements. A whole line has gone down before our machine-guns; then we have a lot of stoppages and they come nearer.

I see one of them, his face upturned, fall into a wire cradle.

His body collapses, his hands remain suspended as though he were praying. Then his body drops clean away and only his hands with the stumps of his arms, shot off, now hang in the wire.

The moment we are about to retreat three faces rise up from the ground in front of us. Under one of the helmets a dark pointed beard and two eyes that are fastened on me. I raise my hand, but I cannot throw into those strange eyes; for one mad moment the whole slaughter whirls like a circus round me, and these two eyes that are alone motionless; then the head rises up, a hand, a movement, and my hand-grenade flies through the air and into him.

We make for the rear, pull wire cradles into the trench and leave bombs behind us with the string pulled, which ensure us a fiery retreat. The machine-guns are already firing from the next position.

We have become wild beasts. We do not fight, we defend ourselves against annihilation. It is not against men that we fling our bombs, what do we know of men in this moment when Death with hands and helmets is hunting us down—now, for the first time in three days we can see his face, now, for the first time in three days we can oppose him; we feel a mad anger. No longer do we lie helpless, waiting on the scaffold, we can destroy and kill, to save ourselves, to save ourselves and be revenged.

We crouch behind every corner, behind every barrier of barbed wire, and hurl heaps of explosives at the feet of the advancing enemy before we run. The blast of the hand-grenades impinges powerfully on our arms and legs; crouching like cats we run on, overwhelmed by this wave that bears us along, that fills us with ferocity, turning us into thugs, into murderers, into God only knows what devils; this wave that multiplies our strength with fear and madness and greed of life, seeking and fighting for nothing but our deliverance. If your own father came over with them you would not hesitate to fling a bomb into him.

• • •

We have lost all feeling for one another. We can hardly control ourselves when our hunted glance lights on the form of some other man. We are insensible, dead men, who through some trick, some dreadful magic, are still able to run and to kill.

A young Frenchman lags behind, he is overtaken, he puts up his hands, in one he still holds his revolver—does he mean to shoot or to give himself up?—a blow from a spade cleaves through his face. A second sees it and tries to run farther; a bayonet jabs into his back. He leaps in the air, his arms thrown wide, his mouth wide open, yelling; he staggers, in his back the bayonet quivers. A third throws away his rifle, cowers down with his hands before his eyes. He is left behind with a few other prisoners to carry off the wounded.

Suddenly in the pursuit we reach the enemy line.

We are so close on the heels of our retreating enemies that we reach it almost at the same time as they. In this way we suffer few casualties. A machine-gun barks, but is silenced with a bomb. Nevertheless, the couple of seconds has sufficed to give us five stomach wounds. With the butt of his rifle Kat smashes to pulp the face of one of the unwounded machine-gunners. We bayonet the others before they have time to get out their bombs. Then thirstily we drink the water they have for cooling the gun.

Liberty Bond Poster by Walter Whitehead from the Collection of the New Jersey Historical Society, Courtesy of American Heritage.

Propaganda in war is often very effective, even when—or especially when—it is unrealistic. What have the artists done in these World

Liberty Bond Poster by F. Strothmann from the Collection of the New Jersey Historical Society, Courtesy of American Heritage.

War One posters to make one soldier brave, strong, and good and the other vicious, cruel, and evil?

Questions

1. Why do you suppose that the rats are called "corpse rats?" Is the incident of the rats just an episode in the soldiers' lives, or does it make a comment on war?

2. Why do the soldiers themselves outlaw the saw-bayonets? Why does the enemy react so violently to those who have these weapons when they are captured?

3. Several pieces of information in the trenches are unspoken and are recognized by signs. How do the soldiers know, for example, that the attack is coming? How do they know when the attack has come?

4. The narrator and his fellow soldiers are clearly human beings with feelings of warmth, sympathy, and fear. Yet they kill and kill brutally. How can you explain their behavior?

5. Do you believe that the soldiers portrayed here would be capable of committing atrocities like those carried out at My Lai?

Composition

1. The episodes of war in these passages are written as if they were a soldier's journal. This narrative device lends the passages a sense of immediacy. Using the present tense, assume the role of a central figure and describe an incident of war. Base your journal on one of the other selections in this book.

2. Read all of Remarque's novel *All Quiet on the Western Front* and Laurence Stallings' and Maxwell Anderson's play *What Price Glory?* Then write an essay comparing and contrasting the portraits of the soldiers at the front. What characteristics does one work leave out that the other builds on? Which takes the more realistic view of war?

Part Two

WAR WITHOUT COMBAT

" 'Tis dangerous when the baser nature comes
Between the pass and fell incensed points
Of mighty opposites"

—HAMLET (v, ii)

1. London

WILLIAM BLAKE

I wander thro' each charter'd street,
Near where the charter'd Thames does flow,
And mark in every face I meet
Marks of weakness, marks of woe.

In every cry of every Man,
In every Infant's cry of fear,
In every voice, in every ban,
The mind-forg'd manacles I hear.

How the Chimney-sweeper's cry
Every black'ning Church appalls;
And the hapless Soldier's sigh
Runs in blood down Palace walls.

But most thro' midnight streets I hear
How the youthful Harlot's curse
Blasts the new born Infant's tear,
And blights with plagues the Marriage hearse.

Questions

1.   This poem was written in 1793 during the reign of King George III, a period of almost constant war for England. This poem has meaning on many levels, and one of these levels is certainly concerned with wartime London. What does the speaker see in the city, and how are the things he sees related? Can you detect his attitude toward wartime London?

2.   Why does Blake repeat the word "charter'd" in the opening lines? Why does he use "mark" three times in two different senses in the first stanza? Are these repetitions and shifting of meaning weaknesses in the poem, or do they make a positive contribution to it?

3.   Who are identified as the chief oppressors? Are the people in any way culpable for their misery? Consider some of these problems: Does "mind-forg'd manacles" indicate a kind of brainwashing, or is the mind in question that of the oppressed which forges its own manacles? Is there any significance to the fact that the speaker perceives weakness *before* woe in the first stanza? Does the Chimney-sweeper, by his acquiescence, "whitewash" the corrupt Church? ("Appall" comes from a Middle English word which meant "to make pale.")

4.   How do you interpret the last two lines of the third stanza? Is the blood necessarily the soldier's? Why is he hapless, and why does he sigh? Why does the blood run down *palace* walls?

Composition

1.   In modern, limited warfare—like that in Korea and Vietnam— American cities and towns have not been as obviously affected by the fight going on across the seas as they were during the First and Second World Wars when posters, blackouts, honor rolls, and the like were constant reminders that the nation was at war. Nevertheless, to the careful observer, there are always signs of war in home-front cities and towns. Write a description of a modern wartime American city or town. What details, actions, and events speak of war?

2. Effigy of War

KAY BOYLE

The barman at the big hotel on the sea front had been an officer in the Italian army during the last war, and somehow or other the rumor began to get around. Whether it was that he said too much to people who spoke his own language with him, saying late at night that the vines in Italy were like no other vines and the voices more musical and the soldiers as good as any others, no matter what history had to say about them, or whether it got around in some other way, it was impossible to know. But the story came to the director of the hotel (Cannes, it was, and the people just as gaudily dressed as other years, and the shops on the Croisette as fancy), and because of the feeling that ran high against the foreigner and against the name of Italy, the director stepped into the lounge bar about eleven one morning to tell the barman what he'd better do. He was a dressy, expensive-looking little man, the director, who could speak four languages with ease, and he had been a Russian once, a White Russian, so that France was the only country left to him now. He came into the bar at a quiet hour, just before the idle would begin wandering in out of the eternally springtime sun, and he jerked his cuffs inside his morning coat and screwed the soft, sagging folds of his throat from his collar wings and started speaking quietly over the mahogany-colored bar.

"Maestro," he said to the barman who had been ten years with them, "with all this trouble going on the management would quite understand your wanting to go back to Italy."

"Italy?" the barman said, and it might have been Siberia he was pronouncing as a destination and the look in his eyes was as startled. He stopped whatever it was he had been doing, setting the glasses straight or putting the ash trays out or the olives, and he looked at the director. He was a slight, dark man and his face was as delicate-boned as a monkey's, and the hair was oiled down flat upon his monkey-fragile skull.

"A lot of Italians are going back," the director said, and he swung himself up onto the stool as elegantly and lightly as a dwarf dressed up for a public appearance, the flesh hairless and pink, and the hand on the wood of the bar as plump as a child's. "Give me a glass of milk," he said, and he went on saying in a lower voice: "In times like these everyone wants to avoid all the trouble they can. Everybody likes to feel he's in his own country." He said it with a slight Russian accent, and the barman waited while the director took the cigarette out of the silver case, and then the barman snapped the lighter open and held the flame to the end of the cigarette in his dark, monkey-nervous hand. "We're perfectly willing to discuss things with you," the director said, and as the first bluish breath of smoke drifted between them, their eyes met for a moment across it, and the director was the first to look away.

"Ah, if we should all go back to the places we belong to!" the barman said as he put the lighter into the pocket of his starched white coat. He turned aside to take the bottle of milk off the ice, and he went on saying in strangely poetic sorrow: "If we all returned to the waters of our own seas and the words of our own languages, France would be left a wilderness—"

"Of course, there are some national exceptions," the director added quickly. "There are some nationalities which cannot go back." He took a swallow of milk and looked rather severely at the barman. "In countries where there have been revolutions, economic up-heavals," he went on, his hand with the cigarette in it making the vague, comprehensive gestures of unrest. "But with Italians," he said, and the barman suddenly leaned forward and laid his small bony hands down flat upon the bar.

"Well, me," he said, "I've been fifteen years in this country.

I'm too old to go back now. For me, Mussolini was an economic up-heaval," he said. He picked up the bottle of milk again and filled the director's glass, pouring it out a little too quickly. "I've never gone back, not since fifteen years," he said, the words spoken sharply and rapidly, almost breathlessly across the bar. "I'm like a refugee, like a political refugee," he said. "I haven't the right to go back."

"That can be taken care of," the director said, and he took out his folded handkerchief and dabbed at the drops of milk on his up-per lip. "The management would advance you what you needed to get back, write you a good testimonial—"

"I haven't done military service for them," the barman said, and he was smiling in something like pain at the director, the grin pulled queer and ancient as a monkey's across his face. "I can't go back," he said. "This is my country by now. If I can't go on working here I can't work anywhere. I wouldn't leave this country no matter what anybody said to me or no matter what they did to me."

"You never did very much about getting any papers out," said the director. He was looking straight ahead at the small silk flags of all the nations and at his own immaculately preserved reflection in the glass. "You never did much about trying to change your nation-ality," he said, and he took another discreet swallow of milk. "You should have thought of that before."

"I might have been a Frenchman today if it hadn't been for my wife," the barman said, and his tongue ran eagerly out along his lip. "My wife—" he said, and he leaned closer, the starched sleeves, with the hairy, bony little wrists showing, laid on the bar. "I haven't seen her for fifteen years," he said, and the director looked at the glass of milk and shrugged his shoulders. "She's in Italy, and she wouldn't sign the papers. She wouldn't do that one thing," he said, the eyes dark and bright, and the face lit suddenly, like a poet's with eagerness and pain. "Not that she wanted me," he said. "It wasn't that. But women like that, Italian women, they're as soft and beauti-ful as flowers and as stubborn as weeds." He said it in abrupt poetic violence, and the director stirred a little uneasily and finished the milk in his glass.

"Now, you take a run up to the Italian Consul this afternoon and have a talk with him," he said, and he wiped his upper lip with his folded handkerchief again. "Tell him you're thinking of going back. Put Raymond on duty for the afternoon. And another thing, Maestro," he said as he got down off the bar stool, "Don't keep that

Corriere della Sera out there where everybody can see it. Put it in your pocket and read it when you get home," he said.

It might have passed off quietly enough like that if the Dane hadn't come into it. He was a snub-nosed, sun-blacked, blond-headed little man who gave swimming lessons in one of the bathing establishments on the beach. He had been a long time there, walking season after season tough and cocky up and down the beach with his chest high and his thumbs hooked into the white belt of his bathing trunks. He wore a bright clean linen cap down to his yellow brows, and royal-blue swimming shorts, and the muscles in his shoulders and arms were as thick and smooth as taffy. But after the war came, he didn't parade up and down the esplanade in the same way in the sun, but stayed hour after hour in the water or else in a corner of the beach café. He still gave lessons, but he let the pupils seek him out in the shade of the café, as if the eyes of the mobilized and the uniformed and the envious could see him less distinctly there.

The one who started it all was the Greek waiter in the big hotel who had got his French naturalization papers eight months before and was leaving for training camp in a week or two. He'd lean over the diners—what was left of the English and the American colony, and the dukes and duchesses, and the Spanish who had got their jewels and their pelts and their money out of Spain—and he'd say:

"What nationality do you think I am, eh? What country would you say I come from?" showing his teeth in pride and pleasure at them as he slipped the dishes of *filets de soles bonne femme* or *champignons à la Reine d'Angleterre* down before them, provided the maître d'hôtel was looking the other way. Sometimes the guests would say he looked one thing, and sometimes another: Italian, Rumanian, or even Argentine, and he'd smile like a prima donna at them, leaning almost on their shoulders, with his eyes shining and the serviette flung rather wildly over his arm.

"No, no, oh, *mon dieu,* no!" he'd say. "I'm pure French. What do you think of that? In another two or three months you'll see me coming in here with gold stripes on my sleeve, ordering everything like everybody else has to eat." And then he'd take out his mobilization order and show it to them, balancing the *homard à l'américaine* on its platter in the other hand as he opened out the stamped, signed paper. "I'm French," he'd say, with the garlic hanging on his breath. "I'm going right into the French army to fight. I'm going to fight for everybody sitting here having dinner tonight," he'd say, and he'd give the people at the next table their salad, holding his mobilization order open in his hand.

The Greek waiter had never liked the look of the Dane, and now that he had his military orders he couldn't so much as stand the sight of the cold-eyed, golden little man. In the hours he had off in the afternoons, he took the habit of walking out on the esplanade and stopping just above the bathing place to call the names down to him. There he would be, the Dane, with his white cap on and his royal-blue bathing trunks, talking half naked to the half naked girls or women on the beach, war or no war, and going on making money just the same.

"Sale étranger!" the Greek would call down, with a fine Greek accent to it, and *"Crepule!"* with his voice ringing out like an opera singer's across the sand and the striped bathing houses and the sea. "France for the French!" he'd roar over the railing, and the little Dane in his bathing suit would go quietly on with his swimming lessons, or if he were alone he'd turn and go into the beach café and sit down out of sight in the shade. There was a week ahead still before the Greek waiter would go, and all those days in the afternoons he'd stand on the esplanade and call the names down. In the end he appealed to the French themselves, exhorting them to rise. "The French for the French!" he'd shout down through the funnel of his hands. "Don't employ foreigners! Give a Frenchman the job!"

The last night of the week the little Dane came into the lounge bar for a drink before he went to bed; coming late, in discretion, when no one else was there. The two of them were talking there together, the Dane sitting on the stool with the glass of beer before him, and the Italian on the other side with his starched jacket on and the wisps of his monkey hair slicked flat across his skull, and in a few minutes the barman would have taken the bottles down and locked the safes and turned the lights out, and then nothing would have occurred. But now the barman was leaning on the counter, speaking the French tongue in a low, rather grievous voice to the swimming teacher, his thin hand rocking from side to side like a little boat as he talked.

"Drinking has ceased," he was saying in faultless pentameter, "in the old way it has ceased. Even before September there was a difference, as if the thirst of man had been slaked at last. To any sensitive eye, the marks of death were to be seen for years on the façades of casinos, palace hotels, luxury restaurants, and on the terraces of country clubs and vast private estates. Even the life of the big bars has been dying," he said. "For years now that I can remember, the lounge bar has been passing through the agonies of death." He made a tragic and noble gesture toward the empty leather armchairs in the half-darkened room, and he said in a low, dreamy voice: "All this is finished. There is no more place in the hearts of men for this kind of thing. The race that insisted on this atmosphere of redundance for its pleasure, that demanded this futility, is vanishing, dying—"

"War levels the ranks," the Dane said quietly. His sun-blacked, sun-withered face under the bright light thatch of hair was as immobile as if carved from wood.

"Ah, before the war even," the barman said softly, and then he stopped, for the men had come into the bar. The Greek waiter walked a little ahead of the others, wearing a gray jersey and a cap pulled down, and they both of them knew him; it was the others behind him they had never seen before.

"Get that one, the one on the stool," the Greek waiter said, and one of the other men stepped past him and walked toward the bar. Just before he got there he lifted his right arm and hit the swimming teacher on the chin. The little, light-crowned head and the strong, small body rose clear of the stool an instant, like a piece of paper lifted and spun sidewise by the wind, and then it sailed into the corner and collapsed there, bent double, by the leather chair. "That's the kind of language he understands," the Greek said, and he crossed the length of thick, soft carpet, jerking his cap up on his forehead. He was smiling with delight when he kicked the swimming teacher's body into another shape. "Walking up and down out there on the beach," the Greek said, and he turned back to the others and the Italian barman behind the bar. "Giving lessons just like men weren't bleeding their guts out for him and people like him—"

"He volunteered. I tell you that man volunteered," the barman began saying, and his bones were shaking like a monkey's in his skin. "I've seen the paper he got. I know he volunteered to fight like anybody else would—" And when he jumped for the bell the Greek waiter reached over and took him by the collar and his starched white coat and dragged him out across the plates of potato chips and the empty beer bottle and the glass the Dane had been drinking and slung him across the elegant little glass-topped tables into the other corner of the room.

"Pick him up and take him along too," the Greek said. "I know all about him I need to know. He was an officer last war, officer in the Italian army, so you'll know what side he'll fight on this time. Take them both out," he said. "This country's not good enough for them, not good enough for either of them."

They did it by moonlight, taking the two men's clothes off on the sand and shingles by the Mediterranean water, and giving it to them in fiercely accelerating violence. They broke the swimming teacher's jaw, and they snapped the arms of the barman behind him like firewood, beating the breath and the life from them with whatever fell under their hands. The Greek carried over a armful of folding iron chairs from the bathing establishment's darkened, abandoned porch and, with these as weapons, they battered the two men's heads down and drove their mouths into the sand.

"So now repeat this after me, foreigners," the Greek began saying in wild holy passion as he kneeled beside them. He had taken the flag out of his jersey and was shaking out its folds. "So now repeat what I'm going to tell you," he said in violent religious fervor against the pulsing and murmuring of the water, and his hands were trembling as he laid the flag out where their mouths could bleed upon the tricolor emblem, the cotton stuff transformed now to the exigencies of a nation and a universe.

Poster, "Enlist," by Fred Spear Imperial War Museum, London with *assistance from Maurice Rickards, author of "Posters of the First World War," New York, 1968.*

On what does this poster base its appeal to enlist and to fight a war? Make your own poster for the Vietnamese war. Advocate either enlistment or draft resistance.

Questions

1. What details does Boyle use to fix your attitude toward the director? Toward the swimming instructor? Toward the Greek-French waiter?

2. Why is the Greek-French waiter hostile toward the Italian barman and, especially, toward the Danish swimming instructor? Are his reasons sound?

3. None of the four characters portrayed is French. Of what significance is this fact in the story?

4. An effigy is a representation or image. Why is Boyle's title appropriate for this story? Taken together, do the title and your response to question No. 2 suggest anything about the author's attitude toward war?

5. On one level, this is a story about the folly of men; on another, it is a story about the folly of Man. Explain the difference. What effect is obtained by calling the flag "cotton stuff" in the last line of the story?

Composition

1. Create your own "effigy of war." Use any medium you wish, but be careful to give your effigy a firm point of view, as Boyle has. A collage would be inexpensive and challenging. For those with equipment, a short film or sounds selected and arranged with sensitivity on a tape recorder could be very powerful. And do not discount writing a short story or an essay that gives a representation of war.

3. The War Prayer

It was a time of great and exalting excitement. The country was up in arms, the war was on, in every breast burned the holy fire of patriotism; the drums were beating, the bands playing, the toy pistols popping, the bunched firecrackers hissing and spluttering; on every hand and far down the receding and fading spread of roofs and balconies a fluttering wilderness of flags flashed in the sun; daily the young volunteers marched down the wide avenue gay and fine in their new uniforms, the proud fathers and mothers and sisters and sweethearts cheering them with voices choked with happy emotion as they swung by; nightly the packed mass meetings listened, panting, to patriot oratory which stirred the deepest deeps of their hearts, and which they interrupted at briefest intervals with cyclones of applause, the tears running down their cheeks the while; in the churches the pastors preached devotion to flag and country, and invoked the God of Battles, beseeching His aid in our good cause in outpouring of fervid eloquence which moved every listener. It was indeed a glad and gracious time, and the half dozen rash spirits that ventured to disapprove of the war and cast a doubt upon its righteousness straightway got such a stern and angry warning that for their personal safety's sake they quickly shrank out of sight and offended no more in that way.

Sunday morning came—next day the battalions would leave for the front; the church was filled; the volunteers were there, their young faces alight with martial dreams—visions of the stern advance, the gathering momentum, the rushing charge, the flashing sabers, the flight of the foe, the tumult, the enveloping smoke, the fierce pursuit, the surrender!—then home from the war, bronzed heroes, welcomed, adored, submerged in golden seas of glory! With the volunteers sat their dear ones, proud, happy, and envied by the neighbors and friends who had no sons and brothers to send forth to the field of honor, there to win for the flag, or, failing, die the noblest of noble deaths. The service proceeded; a war chapter from the Old Testament was read; the first prayer was said; it was followed by an organ burst that shook the building, and with one impulse the house rose, with glowing eyes and beating hearts, and poured out that tremendous invocation—

"God the all-terrible! Thou who ordainest, Thunder thy clarion and lightning thy sword!"

Then came the "long" prayer. None could remember the like of it for passionate pleading and moving and beautiful language. The burden of its supplication was, that an ever-merciful and benignant Father of us all would watch over our noble young soldiers, and aid, comfort, and encourage them in their patriotic work; bless them, shield them in the day of battle and the hour of peril, bear them in His mighty hand, make them strong and confident, invincible in the bloody onset; help them to crush the foe, grant to them and to their flag and country imperishable honor and glory—

An aged stranger entered and moved with slow and noiseless step up the main aisle, his eyes fixed upon the minister, his long body clothed in a robe that reached to his feet, his head bare, his white hair descending in a frothy cataract to his shoulders, his seamy face unnaturally pale, pale even to ghastliness. With all eyes following him and wondering, he made his silent way; without pausing, he ascended to the preacher's side and stood there, waiting. With shut lids the preacher, unconscious of his presence, continued his moving prayer, and at last finished it with the words, uttered in fervent appeal, "Bless our arms, grant us the victory, O Lord our God, Father and Protector of our land and flag!"

The stranger touched his arm, motioned him to step aside—which the startled minister did—and took his place. During some moments he surveyed the spellbound audience with solemn eyes, in which burned an uncanny light; then in a deep voice he said:

"I come from the Throne—bearing a message from Almighty God!" The words smote the house with a shock; if the stranger perceived it he gave no attention. "He has heard the prayer of His servant your shepherd, and will grant it if such shall be your desire after I, His messenger, shall have explained to you its import—that is to say, its full import. For it is like unto many of the prayers of men, in that it asks for more than he who utters it is aware of—except he pause and think.

"God's servant and yours has prayed his prayer. Has he paused and taken thought? Is it one prayer? No, it is two—one uttered, the other not. Both have reached the ear of Him Who heareth all supplications, the spoken and the unspoken. Ponder this—keep it in mind. If you would beseech a blessing upon yourself, beware! lest without intent you invoke a curse upon a neighbor at the same time. If you pray for the blessing of rain upon your crop which needs it, by that act you are possibly praying for a curse upon some neighbor's crop which may not need rain and can be injured by it.

"You have heard your servant's prayer—the uttered part of it. I am commissioned of God to put into words the other part of it— that part which the pastor—and also you in your hearts—fervently prayed silently. And ignorantly and unthinkingly? God grant that it was so! You heard these words: 'Grant us the victory, O Lord our God!' That is sufficient. The *whole* of the uttered prayer is compact into those pregnant words. Elaborations were not necessary. When you have prayed for victory you have prayed for many unmentioned results which follow victory—*must* follow it, cannot help but follow it. Upon the listening spirit of God the Father fell also the unspoken part of the prayer. He commandeth me to put it into words. Listen!

"O Lord our Father, our young patriots, idols of our hearts, go forth to battle—be Thou near them! With them—in spirit—we also go forth from the sweet peace of our beloved firesides to smite the foe. O Lord our God, help us to tear their soldiers to bloody shreds with our shells; help us to cover their smiling fields with the pale forms of their patriot dead; help us to drown the thunder of the guns with the shrieks of their wounded, writhing in pain; help us to lay waste their humble homes with a hurricane of fire; help us to wring the hearts of their unoffending widows with unavailing grief; help us to turn them out roofless with their little children to wander un-friended the wastes of their desolated land in rags and hunger and thirst, sports of the sun flames of summer and the icy winds of winter, broken in spirit, worn with travail, imploring Thee for the refuge of the grave and denied it—for our sakes who adore Thee, Lord, blast their hopes, blight their lives, protract their bitter pilgrimage, make heavy their steps, water their way with their tears, stain the white snow with the blood of their wounded feet! We ask it, in the spirit of love, of Him Who is the Source of Love, and Who is the ever-faithful refuge and friend of all that are sore beset and seek His aid with humble and contrite hearts. Amen."

(*After a pause.*) "Ye have prayed it; if ye still desire it, speak! The messenger of the Most High waits."

It was believed afterward that the man was a lunatic, because there was no sense in what he said.

Questions

1.   In this tale, we are given two views of war by a narrator who ostensibly reports what happens without commenting on it. With which view does he sympathize? How does he let us know? Is the reason given in the last sentence the author's belief, merely a piece of reportage, or something more?

2.   Irony is an important tool in this story. What, for example, is ironic about the entire situation of praying for a victory in war? When is the irony of this situation first suggested? When does it become obvious?

3.   Who or what is the old man? Why is he branded a lunatic? (Try to look deeper than the explicit reason.)

4.   Why do the people in the church regard it as an honor to have a husband or son going to war? Does it matter that the causes of this war are never revealed in the story? What American wars could be called "just wars"?

Composition

1.   Rewrite Twain's "The War Prayer" as a script for radio. Include sound effects and music. You might develop briefly one or two characters and add some dialogue. When the script is written, try producing the play on audio tape. Several members of the class might work together on this project.

2.   "The War Prayer," Johnson's speech on Vietnam (p. 169), and Wald's "A Generation in Search of a Future" (p. 185) are entirely or mainly speeches. Using these selections or other well-known speeches, create on tape or for live, dramatic presentation a series of speeches that makes a statement about war. Poems like "The Mother" (p. 83) or "Patterns" (p. 99) can be used too, since they are essentially dramatic. Several members of the class can participate in this task, each assuming a different role. One student could provide between the speeches narrative links written by the student participants. An excellent resource for this project is *A Treasury of the World's Great Speeches,* revised edition, edited by Houston Peterson, New York: Simon and Schuster, 1965.

4. *The Mother*

PADRAIC PEARSE

I do not grudge them; Lord, I do not grudge
My two strong sons that I have seen go out
To break their strength and die, they and a few,
In bloody protest for a glorious thing.
They shall be spoken of among their people,
The generations shall remember them,
And call them blessed;
But I will speak their names to my own heart
In the long nights;
The little names that were familiar once
Round my dead hearth.
Lord, thou art hard on mothers:
We suffer in their coming and their going;
And tho' I grudge them not, I weary, weary
Of the long sorrow—And yet I have my joy:
My sons were faithful, and they fought.

"The Mother" by Padraic Pearse, from *One Thousand Years of Irish Poetry,* edited by Kathleen Hoagland. Reprinted by permission of The Devon-Adair Company, Old Greenwich, Connecticut, copyright © 1947.

Questions

1. What is the mother's loss, and how does she find consolation for it?

2. In what sense is the mother's acceptance of the nobleness of her sons' deaths a means of self-protection? How well does she understand the cause that she calls "a glorious thing"? Are her feelings consistent throughout the poem? Why does she waver?

3. Could this poem be the response of an American mother who has lost a son in Vietnam? In Korea? In the Second World War? Could it be the response of an Israeli mother or a Palestinian mother who has just lost a son in the Middle East war? In each case, what would the "glorious thing" be?

Composition

1. War and death are inextricably bound together, and death in war is usually the death of the young. Write an essay in which you explore the meaning of a young person's death—in war or not. Try to choose someone specific, either someone you knew or knew about.

5. Hiroshima: August 6, 1945

JOHN HERSEY

The Reverend Mr. Tanimoto got up at five o'clock that morning. He was alone in the parsonage, because for some time his wife had been commuting with their year-old baby to spend nights with a friend in Ushida, a suburb to the north. Of all the important cities of Japan, only two, Kyoto and Hiroshima, had not been visited in strength by *B-san,* or Mr. B. as the Japanese, with a mixture of respect and unhappy familiarity, called the B-29; and Mr. Tanimoto, like all his neighbors and friends, was almost sick with anxiety. He had heard uncomfortably detailed accounts of mass raids on Kure, Iwakuni, Tokuyama, and other nearby towns; he was sure Hiroshima's turn would come soon. He had slept badly the night before, because there had been several air-raid warnings. Hiroshima had been getting such warnings almost every night for weeks, for at that time the B-29s were using Lake Biwa, northeast of Hiroshima, as a rendezvous point, and no matter what city the Americans planned to hit, the Superfortresses streamed in over the coast near Hiroshima. The frequency of the warnings and the continued abstinence of Mr. B with respect to Hiroshima had made its citizens jittery; a rumor was going around that the Americans were saving something special for the city.

Mr. Tanimoto is a small man, quick to talk, laugh, and cry. He wears his black hair parted in the middle and rather long; the prominence of the frontal bones just above his eyebrows and the smallness of his mustache, mouth, and chin give him a strange, old-young look, boyish and yet wise, weak and yet fiery. He moves nervously and fast, but with a restraint which suggests that he is a cautious, thoughtful man. He showed, indeed, just those qualities in the uneasy days before the bomb fell. Besides having his wife spend the nights in Ushida, Mr. Tanimoto had been carrying all the portable things from his church, in the close-packed residential district called Nagaragawa, to a house that belonged to a rayon manufacturer in Koi, two miles from the center of town. The rayon man, a Mr. Matsui, had opened his then unoccupied estate to a large number of his friends and acquaintances, so that they might evacuate whatever they wished to a safe distance from the probable target area. Mr. Tanimoto had had no difficulty in moving chairs, hymnals, Bibles, altar gear, and church records by pushcart himself, but the organ console and an upright piano required some aid. A friend of his named Matsuo had, the day before, helped him get the piano out to Koi; in return, he had promised this day to assist Mr. Matsuo in hauling out a daughter's belongings. That is why he had risen so early.

Mr. Tanimoto cooked his own breakfast. He felt awfully tired. The effort of moving the piano the day before, a sleepless night, weeks of worry and unbalanced diet, the cares of his parish—all combined to make him feel hardly adequate to the new day's work. There was another thing, too: Mr. Tanimoto had studied theology at Emory University, in Atlanta, Georgia; he had graduated in 1940; he spoke excellent English; he dressed in American clothes; he had corresponded with many American friends right up to the time the war began; and among a people obsessed with a fear of being spied upon—perhaps almost obsessed himself—he found himself growing increasingly uneasy. The police had questioned him several times, and just a few days before, he had heard that an influential acquaintance, a Mr. Tanaka, a retired officer of the Toyo Kisen Kaisha steamship line, an anti-Christian, a man famous in Hiroshima for his showy philanthropies and notorious for his personal tyrannies, had been telling people that Tanimoto should not be trusted. In compensation, to show himself publicly a good Japanese, Mr. Tanimoto had taken on the chairmanship of his local *tonarigumi*, or Neighborhood Association, and to his other duties and concerns this position had added the business of organizing air-raid defense for about twenty families.

Before six o'clock that morning, Mr. Tanimoto started for Mr. Matsuo's house. There he found that their burden was to be a *tansu,* a large Japanese cabinet, full of clothing and household goods. The two men set out. The morning was perfectly clear and so warm that the day promised to be uncomfortable. A few minutes after they started, the air-raid siren went off—a minute-long blast that warned of approaching planes but indicated to the people of Hiroshima only a slight degree of danger, since it sounded every morning at this time, when an American weather plane came over. The two men pulled and pushed the handcart through the city streets. Hiroshima was a fan-shaped city, lying mostly on the six islands formed by the seven estuarial rivers that branch out from the Ota River; its main commercial and residential districts, covering about four square miles in the center of the city, contained three-quarters of its population, which had been reduced by several evacuation programs from a wartime peak of 380,000 to about 245,000. Factories and other residential districts, or suburbs, lay compactly around the edges of the city. To the south were the docks, an airport, and the island-studded Inland Sea. A rim of mountains runs around the other three sides of the delta. Mr. Tanimoto and Mr. Matsuo took their way through the shopping center, already full of people, and across two of the rivers to the sloping streets of Koi, and up them to the out-skirts and foothills. As they started up a valley away from the tight-ranked houses, the all-clear sounded. (The Japanese radar operators, detecting only three planes, supposed that they comprised a recon-naissance.) Pushing the handcart up to the rayon man's house was tiring, and the men, after they had maneuvered their load into the driveway and to the front steps, paused to rest awhile. They stood with a wing of the house between them and the city. Like most homes in this part of Japan, the house consisted of a wooden frame and wooden walls supporting a heavy tile roof. Its front hall, packed with rolls of bedding and clothing, looked like a cool cave full of fat cushions. Opposite the house, to the right of the front door, there was a large, finicky rock garden. There was no sound of planes. The morning was still; the place was cool and pleasant.

Then a tremendous flash of light cut across the sky. Mr. Tanimoto has a distinct recollection that it travelled from east to west, from the city toward the hills. It seemed a sheet of sun. Both he and Mr. Matsuo reacted in terror—and both had time to react (for they were 3,500 yards, or two miles, from the center of the explosion). Mr. Matsuo dashed up the front steps into the house and dived among the bedrolls and buried himself there. Mr. Tanimoto took four to five steps and threw himself between two big rocks in the garden. He bellied up very hard against one of them. As his face was against the stone, he did not see what happened. He felt a sudden pressure, and then splinters and pieces of board and fragments of tile fell on him. He heard no roar. (Almost no one in Hiroshima recalls hearing any noise of the bomb. But a fisherman in his sampan on the Inland Sea near Tsuzu, the man with whom Mr. Tanimoto's mother-in-law and sister-in-law were living, saw the flash and heard a tremendous explosion; he was nearly twenty miles from Hiroshima, but the thunder was greater than when the B-29s hit Iwakuni, only five miles away.)

When he dared, Mr. Tanimoto raised his head and saw that the rayon man's house had collapsed. He thought a bomb had fallen directly on it. Such clouds of dust had risen that there was a sort of twilight around. In panic, not thinking for the moment of Mr. Matsuo under the ruins, he dashed out into the street. He noticed as he ran that the concrete wall of the estate had fallen over—toward the house rather than away from it. In the street, the first thing he saw was a squad of soldiers who had been burrowing into the hillside opposite, making one of the thousands of dugouts in which the Japanese apparently intended to resist invasion, hill by hill, life for life; the soldiers were coming out of the hole, where they should have been safe, and blood was running from their heads, chests, and backs. They were silent and dazed.

Under what seemed to be a local dust cloud, the day grew darker and darker.

• • •

After the bombing, Mr. Tanimoto made his way to Asano Park along the River Ota in Hiroshima.

• • •

Just before dark, Mr. Tanimoto came across a twenty-year-old girl, Mrs. Kamai, the Tanimoto's next-door neighbor. She was crouching on the ground with the body of her infant daughter in her arms.

The baby had evidently been dead all day. Mrs. Kamai jumped up when she saw Mr. Tanimoto and said, "Would you please try to locate my husband?"

Mr. Tanimoto knew that her husband had been inducted into the Army just the day before; he and Mrs. Tanimoto had entertained Mrs. Kamai in the afternoon, to make her forget. Kamai had reported to the Chugoku Regional Army Headquarters—near the ancient castle in the middle of town—where some four thousand troops were stationed. Judging by the many maimed soldiers Mr. Tanimoto had seen during the day, he surmised that the barracks had been badly damaged by whatever it was that had hit Hiroshima. He knew he hadn't a chance of finding Mrs. Kamai's husband, even if he searched, but he wanted to humor her. "I'll try," he said.

"You've got to find him," she said. "He loved our baby so much. I want him to see her once more."

. . .

Mr. Tanimoto found about twenty men and women on the sandspit. He drove the boat onto the bank and urged them to get aboard. They did not move and he realized that they were too weak to lift themselves. He reached down and took a woman by the hands, but her skin slipped off in huge, glove-like pieces. He was so sickened by this that he had to sit down for a moment. Then he got out into the water and, though a small man, lifted several of the men and women, who were naked, into his boat. Their backs and breasts were clammy, and he remembered uneasily what the great burns he had seen during the day had been like: yellow at first, then red and swollen, with the skin sloughed off, and finally, in the evening, suppurated and smelly. With the tide risen, his bamboo pole was now too short and he had to paddle most of the way across with it. On the other side, at a higher spit, he lifted the slimy living bodies out and carried them up the slope away from the tide. He had to keep consciously repeating to himself, "These are human beings." It took him three trips to get them all across the river. When he had finished, he decided he had to have a rest, and he went back to the park.

As Mr. Tanimoto stepped up the dark bank, he tripped over someone, and someone else said angrily, "Look out! That's my hand." Mr. Tanimoto, ashamed of hurting wounded people, embarrassed at being able to walk upright, suddenly thought of the naval hospital ship, which had not come (it never did), and he had for a moment a feeling of blind, murderous rage at the crew of the ship, and then at all doctors. Why didn't they come to help these people?

• • •

Mr. Tanimoto was still angry at doctors. He decided that he would personally bring one to Asano Park—by the scruff of the neck, if necessary. He crossed the river, went past the Shinto shrine where he had met his wife for a brief moment the day before, and walked to the East Parade Ground. Since this had long before been designated as an evacuation area, he thought he would find an aid station there. He did find one, operated by an Army medical unit, but he also saw that its doctors were hopelessly overburdened, with thousands of patients sprawled among corpses across the field in front of it. Nevertheless, he went up to one of the Army doctors and said, as reproachfully as he could, "Why have you not come to Asano Park? You are badly needed there."

Without even looking up from his work, the doctor said in a tired voice, "This is my station."

"But there are many dying on the riverbank over there."

"The first duty," the doctor said, "is to take care of the slightly wounded."

"Why—when there are many who are heavily wounded on the riverbank?"

The doctor moved to another patient. "In an emergency like this," he said, as if he were reciting from a manual, "the first task is to help as many as possible—to save as many lives as possible. There is no hope for the heavily wounded. They will die. We can't bother with them."

"That may be right from a medical standpoint—" Mr. Tanimoto began, but then he looked out across the field, where the many dead lay close and intimate with those who were still living, and he turned away without finishing his sentence, angry now with himself. He didn't know what to do; he had promised some of the dying people in the park that he would bring them medical aid. They might die feeling cheated. He saw a ration stand at one side of the field, and he went to it and begged some rice cakes and biscuits, and he took them back, in lieu of doctors, to the people in the park.

1940 Pulitzer Prize-Winning Cartoon—Reprinted from the Chicago Sunday Times of June 2, 1940.

1940 Pulitzer Prize-Winning Cartoon by Jacob Burck—Reprinted from the Chicago Sunday Times of June 2, 1940.

It is June, 1940. All over the world people are in trouble. They don't know where to turn or what to do for help. Soldiers are dying; so are countries; men and women are suffering. Nothing seems safe anymore. Even the Maginot line is gone. And I am trying to draw a cartoon for tomorrow.

Before me are vague lines and scribbles forming shapes on a piece of paper. One of the shapes becomes a mother, a mother crying. Other shapes become the bombed ruins of her house. Certain lines show ruthless bombing planes. War is hard on mothers.

But that is not as simple an idea as it should be for a cartoon. What is simple? A child. The mother becomes a child. The child is getting ready for bed. Alone, her father off to battle, her mother perhaps killed by bombs, the little girl begins to say her prayers:

"Now I lay me down to sleep" . . . *One by one the phrases of the prayer come* . . . *"If I should die before I wake . . ."*

That's it.

"If I should die before I wake" . . . *a little child in trouble turning childlike to God.*

That will be the cartoon for tomorrow.

JACOB BURCK

One may say that this cartoon has an implicit thesis. Try to verbalize it. How do the caption and the pictorial images combine to convey the thesis?

Try your hand at a political-military cartoon. Base your effort on one of the writings in this book or on a contemporary theme. Even if you are not a gifted cartoonist, an exaggerated detail or two can compensate for a lack of realistic representation. As an alternative, gather several photographs from newspapers and magazines. Caption them and arrange them in a series to make a statement about war or another significant contemporary problem.

Questions

1. Was the bombing of Hiroshima surprising or expected? Support your answer by pointing to specific details in the narrative.

2. How do you account for the fact that there seemed to be little panic after the bomb had been dropped? Consider the behavior of Mr. Tanimoto, Mrs. Kamai, and the military doctor.

3. Why does Mr. Tanimoto have to remind himself that the people he is helping are human beings?

Composition

1. The day Mr. Tanimoto describes is historic. It is a day that is likely to be fixed in the minds of people who lived through it whether they were in Hiroshima or Kansas City or New York. Interview some people who remember the day. Then write a paper describing and commenting on their immediate responses to the advent of the atomic age. How important did the bomb seem to them on that day? Did they feel joy? Sadness? Fear? Horror?

6. Document Number 2992-PS

THE TESTIMONY OF HANS GRÄBE AT THE NUREMBERG WAR TRIALS, JULY 27, 1946

"On 5 October 1943 when I visited the building office at Dubno my foreman . . . told me that in the vicinity of the site, Jews from Dubno had been shot in three large pits, each about 30 meters long and 3 meters deep. About 1,500 persons had been killed daily. All of the 5,000 Jews who had still been living in Dubno before the action were to be liquidated. As the shooting had taken place in his presence, he was still much upset.

"Thereupon I drove to the site, accompanied by my foreman, and saw near it great mounds of earth, about 30 meters long and 2 meters high. Several trucks stood in front of the mounds. Armed Ukrainian militia drove the people off the trucks under the supervision of an SS man. The militia men acted as guards on the trucks and drove them to and from the pit. All these people had the regulation yellow patches on the front and back of their clothes and thus could be recognized as Jews.

"My foreman and I went directly to the pits. Nobody bothered us. Now I heard rifle shots in quick succession from behind one of the earth mounds. The people who had got off the trucks—men, women, and children of all ages—had to undress upon the orders of an SS man, who carried a riding or dog whip. They had to put down their clothes in fixed places, sorted according to shoes, top clothing, and underclothing. I saw a heap of shoes of about 800 to 1,000 pairs, great piles of under linen and clothing. Without screaming or weeping these people undressed, stood around in family groups, kissed each other, said farewells, and waited for a sign from another SS man, who stood near the pit, also with a whip in his hand. During the 15 minutes that I stood near I heard no complaint or plea for mercy. I watched a family of about eight persons, a man and a woman both about 50 with their children of about 1, 8, and 10, and two grown-up daughters of about 20 to 24. An old woman with snow-white hair was holding the one-year-old child in her arms and singing to it and tickling it. The child was cooing with delight. The couple were looking on with tears in their eyes. The father was holding the hand of a boy about 10 years old and speaking to him softly; the boy was fighting his tears. The father pointed to the sky, stroked his head, and seemed to explain something to him. At that moment the SS man at the pit shouted something to his comrade. The latter counted off about 20 persons and instructed them to go behind the earth mound. Among them was the family which I have mentioned. I well remember a girl, slim and with black hair, who as she passed close to me, pointed to herself and said, '23'. I walked around the mound and found myself confronted by a tremendous grave. People were closely wedged together and lying on top of each other so that only their heads were visible. Nearly all had blood running over their shoulders from their heads. Some of the people shot were still moving. Some were lifting their arms and turning their heads to show that they were still alive. The pit was already two-thirds full. I estimated that it already contained about 1,000 people. I looked for the man who did the shooting. He was an SS man, who sat at the edge of the narrow end of the pit, his feet dangling into the pit. He had a tommy gun on his knees and was smoking a cigaret. The people, completely naked, went down some steps which were cut in the clay wall of the pit and clambered over the heads of the people lying there, to the place to which the SS man directed them. They lay down in front of the dead or injured people; some caressed those who were still alive and spoke to them in a low voice. Then I heard a series of shots. I looked into the pit and saw that the bodies were twitching or the heads lying motionless on top of the bodies which lay before them. Blood was running away from their necks. I was surprised that I was not ordered away but I saw that there were two or three guards in uniform nearby. The next batch was approaching already. They went down into the pit, lined themselves up against the previous victims and were shot. When I walked back round the mound I noticed another truck load of people which had just arrived. This time it included sick and infirm persons. An old, very thin woman with terribly thin legs was undressed by others who were already naked, while two people held her up. The woman appeared to be paralyzed. The naked people carried the woman around the mound. I left with my foreman and drove in my car back to Dubno.

"On the morning of the next day, when I again visited the site, I saw about 30 naked people lying near the pit—about 30 to 50 meters away from it. Some of them were still alive; they looked straight in front of them with a fixed stare and seemed to notice neither the chilliness of the morning nor the workers of my firm who stood around. A girl of about 20 spoke to me and asked me to give her clothes and help her escape. At that moment we heard a fast car approach and I noticed that it was an SS detail. I moved away to my site. Ten minutes later we heard shots from the vicinity of the pit. The Jews still alive had been ordered to throw the corpses into the pit, then they had themselves to lie down in this to be shot in the neck."

Questions

1. Gräbe tells what happened matter of factly. He does not comment on what he sees; he does not use judgmental adjectives to express his feelings. Would his testimony have been more or less effective had he used words like "horrible," "merciless," "monstrous," and the like?

2. Gräbe's testimony is so grotesque that it is almost unbelievable. What makes his story credible?

3. Which details of his testimony do you find especially moving? Does his selection of details in any way indicate where his sympathies lie?

4. What similarities and differences do you see between the incidents at Dubno and those at My Lai which are described by Seymour Hersh in the last section of this book?

Composition

1. An elegy is a poem that laments someone's death. Try writing a short elegy for the victims at Dubno. Follow Gräbe's example by avoiding many judgmental adjectives or emotive words. Make your details as concrete as possible. Write from a specific point of view— Gräbe's or a survivor's, for example. You might assume the role of an SS man on trial at Nuremberg, looking back at Dubno two years after the fact. To whom might he address his elegy? Taking a different approach, what might the son or daughter of an SS man write to the son or daughter of a victim at Dubno? Do not exclude the possibility of writing from your own point of view after reading the testimony. If you find the demands of writing poetry too taxing, try writing a prose elegy.

7. Patterns

―――――――――

AMY LOWELL

I walk down the garden paths,
And all the daffodils
Are blowing, and the bright blue squills.
I walk down the patterned garden paths
In my stiff, brocaded gown.
With my powdered hair and jeweled fan,
I too am a rare
Pattern. As I wander down
The garden paths.

My dress is richly figured,
And the train
Makes a pink and silver stain
On the gravel, and the thrift
Of the borders.
Just a plate of current fashion,
Tripping by in high-heeled, ribboned shoes.
Not a softness anywhere about me,
Only whalebone and brocade.
And I sink on a seat in the shade

―――――――――

From *The Complete Poetical Works of Amy Lowell,* Houghton Mifflin Company. Reprinted by permission of the publisher.

Of a lime tree. For my passion
Wars against the stiff brocade.
The daffodils and squills
Flutter in the breeze
As they please.
And I weep;
For the lime tree is in blossom
And one small flower has dropped upon my bosom.

And the plashing of waterdrops
In the marble fountain
Comes down the garden paths.
The dripping never stops.
Underneath my stiffened gown
Is the softness of a woman bathing in a marble basin,
A basin in the midst of hedges grown
So thick, she cannot see her lover hiding,
But she guesses he is near,
And the sliding of the water
Seems the stroking of a dear
Hand upon her.
What is Summer in a fine brocaded gown!
I should like to see it lying in a heap upon the ground.
All the pink and silver crumpled up on the ground.

I would be the pink and silver as I ran along the paths,
And he would stumble after,
Bewildered by my laughter.
I should see the sun flashing from his sword-hilt and the buckles
    on his shoes.
I would choose
To lead him in a maze along the patterned paths,
A bright and laughing maze for my heavy-booted lover
Till he caught me in the shade,
And the buttons of his waistcoat bruised my body as he clasped me,
Aching, melting, unafraid.
With the shadows of the leaves and the sundrops,
And the plopping of the waterdrops,
All about us in the open afternoon—
I am very like to swoon
With the weight of this brocade,
For the sun sifts through the shade.

Underneath the fallen blossom
In my bosom
Is a letter I have hid.
It was brought to me this morning by a rider from the Duke.
"Madam, we regret to inform you that Lord Hartwell
Died in action Thursday se'nnight."
As I read it in the white, morning sunlight,
The letters squirmed like snakes.
"Any answer, Madam," said my footman.
"No," I told him.
"See that the messenger takes some refreshment.
No, no answer."
And I walked into the garden,
Up and down the patterned paths,
In my stiff, correct brocade.
The blue and yellow flowers stood up proudly in the sun,
Each one.
I stood upright too,
Held rigid to the pattern
By the stiffness of my gown;
Up and down I walked,
Up and down.

In a month he would have been my husband.
In a month, here, underneath this lime,
We would have broken the pattern;
He for me, and I for him,
He as Colonel, I as Lady,
On this shady seat.
He had a whim
That sunlight carried blessing.
And I answered, "It shall be as you have said."
Now he is dead.

In Summer and in Winter I shall walk
Up and down
The patterned garden paths
In my stiff, brocaded gown.
The squills and daffodils
Will give place to pillared roses, and to asters, and to snow.
I shall go
Up and down

In my gown.
Gorgeously arrayed,
Boned and stayed.
And the softness of my body will be guarded from embrace
By each button, hook, and lace.
For the man who should loose me is dead,
Fighting with the Duke in Flanders,
In a pattern called a war.
Christ! What are patterns for?

Questions

1. The speaker in this poem is a fully realized character. What is she like? What does her self-characterization add to the impact of the poem's last line?

2. What are some of the patterns the woman speaks of? What does she mean when she says: "I too am a rare / Pattern" (ll. 7-8)? What is the pattern she and her lover would have broken (l. 83)? Where in the poem are patterns broken?

3. In what sense is war a pattern?

4. This poem and Padraic Pearse's "The Mother" belie the fantasy that women do not fight and fall in wars. Compare the speakers in these two poems. What, finally, is the attitude of each toward war? In practical terms, which woman can look more hopefully to the future and why? Has either won a greater share of your sympathy than the other?

Composition

1. The notion of war as a pattern suggests the possibility of a visual representation of that pattern. One such representation is the series of three photographs on pages 142-143. Compose your own visual representation of the pattern of war. You might try a collage, a montage, a linear series of photographs, cartoons, or a painting. Let your imagination play with this job.

Part Three

GENERALS AND PHILOSOPHERS

"There is many a boy here today who looks on war as all glory, but, boys it is all hell."

—WILLIAM TECUMSEH SHERMAN

1. The Glories of Our Blood and State

JAMES SHIRLEY

The glories of our blood and state
Are shadows, not substantial things;
There is no armor against fate;
Death lays his icy hand on kings.
Scepter and crown
Must tumble down,
And in the dust be equal made
With the poor crooked scythe and spade.

Some men with swords may reap the field,
And plant fresh laurels where they kill;
But their strong nerves at last must yield,
They tame but one another still.
Early or late,
They stoop to fate,
And must give up their murmuring breath
When they, pale captives, creep to death.

The garlands wither on your brow,
Then boast no more your mighty deeds;
Upon death's purple altar now
See where the victor-victim bleeds.
Your heads must come
To the cold tomb;
Only the actions of the just
Smell sweet and blossom in their dust.

Questions

1.   Rhetorically speaking, Shirley's poem is a piece of persuasive writing addressed ultimately to great rulers and warriors. How would you describe the persona or voice that Shirley assumes? Is his persuasion strong? What details does he use to carry his point?

2.   As the poem progresses from stanza to stanza, the speaker seems to move closer to his audience. What effect does this closing movement have? How does Shirley achieve this effect?

3.   Shirley wrote this poem at a time when virtually all men believed in God and eternal rewards and punishment. Would his admonition be effective in a world like ours, where so many men feel that God is dead?

Composition

1.   Write an essay in which you give advice on war to the leaders of the world today. Try, if you can, to follow Shirley's strategy of moving from general address to direct address.

2. A Soldier's Duty

CURTIS LEMAY
WITH
MACKINLAY KANTOR

If you have a bomber command out in the field, and are a major-general accordingly—And if a scholarly field grade Army engineer officer comes and talks to your people, and presents credentials which indicate that he is on a mission of extreme importance, and that he has highly classified information to present to the commanding general—If you are the commanding general you may be pardoned for thinking that something big is in the wind.

I had never heard of the Manhattan District Project before. I didn't know that any nuclear bombs were in the works. My job had always been to get as many conventional bombs on enemy targets as it was possible to put there. Nothing more than that.

This officer's job was to appear at Guam and tell me about things; and then go on up to Tinian and get the pits built, and the equipment. All facilities constructed, so that we could employ our new ordnance. He didn't give me any TNT equivalents. I didn't know much about this whole thing and didn't ask about it, because it was so hot. Didn't wish to have any more information than it was necessary for me to have.

But I knew that the bomb was coming out there, and I knew that

From *MISSION WITH LeMAY: MY STORY* by Curtis E. LeMay with MacKinlay Kantor. Copyright © 1965 by Curtis E. LeMay and MacKinlay Kantor. Reprinted by permission of Doubleday & Company, Inc.

it was going to be our job to drop it. And I was told that it was a nuclear weapon. That didn't make too much of an impression: my college physics course was a long way behind. Generally speaking, I could understand what the Army man was talking about. We had a very powerful weapon. But it was late in the war, and I was busy. Rapidly we were wiping out Japanese industry with incendiaries— when we could get them in sufficient quantity.

So Colonel Manhattan District went on up to Tinian to get the place set up. Let me say this: it was one of the best-kept military secrets of the war.

The President and his Interim Committee had approved the use of these bombs, and 21st Bomber Command's responsibility was to see that they were used with the utmost competence. To begin with, we had to have a fresh target—at least a target whereon no great destructive capacity had yet been exerted. None of the burned-up towns would do. Tokyo wouldn't do. There would be no possible way to measure the new bomb's effectiveness against a landscape of cinders.

As early as the first week of July we received orders not to direct any attacks against Kyoto, Hiroshima, Kokura or Niigata. Later on they removed Kyoto from this list, and substituted Nagasaki. Kyoto was the ancient capital of Japan. Just as in the European war: if you'd have had a choice between Heidelberg and Mannheim, you would have razed Mannheim.

The essential annihilative capacity of the new weapon (or weapons, rather; two distinct types of atomic bombs were already in existence; and one was used against Hiroshima and the other against Nagasaki) was not known in exactitude. They didn't shoot that one off down there in the desert until the 16th of July. Until that date everything had been theoretical. Even after the eventual detonation, we *supposed* that it would knock the hell out of a town. Nobody knew exactly what it would do. The bomb had never been used in warfare.

If you judge from all the articles and editorials which have been written in the past twenty years, and all the prayers which have been prayed, and all the mourning and preaching that has been going on, you would judge that we crossed some kind of moral boundary with the use of these weapons. The assumption seems to be that it is much more wicked to kill people with a nuclear bomb, than to kill people by busting their heads with rocks. St. Stephen, in the

Bible, was stoned to death—just as prostitutes had been stoned, before Christ came along and was kind to Mary Magdalene.

There are a select group of writers, clergymen, savants, and self-appointed philosophers, and a not-so-select group of youthful or agèd beatniks, who are ready to support any antimilitary demonstration in any clime or country, at any time of the day or night. These mooncalves would have you convinced that a big bang is far wickeder than a little bang. I suppose they believe also that a machine gun is a hundred times wickeder than a bow and arrow. I've been shot at with machine guns . . . haven't, to my knowledge, ever been shot at with a bow and arrow. If I'd been killed, I don't suppose it would have made much difference to me which weapon was used.

Actually we, in the bombardment business, were not at all concerned about this. That doesn't mean that we were more bloodthirsty than other folks. We just weren't bothered about the morality of the question. If we could shorten the war we wanted to shorten it.

Most of us in the Army Air Forces had been convinced for a long time that it would be possible to defeat the Japanese without invading their home islands. We needed to establish bases within reasonable range; then we could bomb and burn them until they quit. That was our theory, and history has proved that we were right. The ground-gripping Army, and the Navy, didn't agree. They discounted the whole idea.

They were getting set for that invasion. Americans were going to have to land on Kyushu and operate against millions of well-trained men. Adequate demonstration of how the cornered Japanese would and could fight, had been offered every time the U.S. forces made a landing in that war. The number of American casualties which would be incurred by an actual invasion of the islands of Kyushu and Honshu was well up in the imaginative brackets and then some.

Therefore, when informed that we were about to be given a piece of ordnance which would far surpass in accomplishment any bomb ever dropped before by any nation, we all said *Swell*. I think we would have won the war anyway, merely by sticking to our incendiary tactics. But we were given the bombs and told to go ahead and drop them.

If a nuclear weapon shortened the war by only a week, probably it saved more lives than were taken by that single glare of heat and radiation. Matter of fact, one time I was asked this same question in Japan, at a press conference. And that was the answer I gave. The

Japanese reaction was all to the good. They believed along with me that it was a question of military expediency and not a moral issue.

I don't mean to imply that, in 1945, there were any editorials in the Japanese press saying what a nice guy I was. As far back as March and April the Tokyo broadcasters had declared me to be a "bloodthirsty maniac" and "wanton killer." One of the Japanese broadcasters spoke as follows:

"Beneath a photograph of unkempt and scowling Gen. LeMay, a leading Tokyo journal called the attention of its readers to his bloodthirsty career. The article said that, only a lieutenant in the United States Air Forces in 1938, he was promoted to major-general and was placed in command of the United States heavy bombers attacking Germany. It said it was none other than LeMay who reduced Hamburg to ashes."

. . . Guess that would be news to the RAF.

Also another commentator complained bitterly, because I had not held to the same pattern of tactics all along. "The enemy planes are closing over our heads with changing tactics. In the types of bombs too, the enemy is challenging us with new weapons we failed to anticipate. Consequently, when we expected the enemy would use only oil bombs, he suddenly raids us with large phosphorous and electronic incendiaries."

So the Japanese press and commentators were somewhat disturbed by our attacks, you can say, long before we ever brought the first atomic bomb over their mainland and kicked it loose.

Actually I think it's more immoral to use *less* force than necessary, than it is to use *more*. If you use less force, you kill off more of humanity in the long run, because you are merely protracting the struggle.

We have had the same situation all over again, both in Korea and in Viet Nam. I suggested informally, when the Korean flap started in 1950, that we go up north immediately with incendiaries and delete four or five of the largest towns: Wonsan, Pyongyang and so on.

The answer from Washington: "No, no, that's too utterly horrible! You'd kill a lot of noncombatants!"

Thus we went along, allowing ourselves to be cajoled into conducting a war under wraps, because the alternative was unacceptable morally. And what happened? We burned down just about every city in North Korea and South Korea *both,* including Pusan.

That one was an accident. But we nearly burned all of it down just the same.

And during the three years of warfare we killed off over a million civilian Koreans and drove several million more from their homes, with the inevitable additional tragedies bound to ensue. The military casualties on both sides totaled nearly three and one-half million.

Over fifty-four thousand dead Americans. . . .

To expunge a few people to stop a war right at the start is unacceptable. Or a few hundred people, or a few thousand. Or—go all out on it—a few hundred thousand. But over a long period of time, wearily killing them off and killing them off, killing millions under the most horrible circumstances—That is acceptable. Mankind keeps on doing it.

Even the crews who freighted the ordnance up to Hiroshima and Nagasaki, and dumped it, didn't know just what they really had. Nobody was sure about the destructive capacity, not even the scientists. When that first bomb went off, and there was a gigantic flare, a burst brighter than the sun, a mushroom-shaped cloud of smoke— They were understandably bowled over by what they witnessed.

That's when a few individuals began to lie awake nights, debating in their own minds the ethical responsibility involved. . . . We had some men over in Europe who went loco just from dropping ordinary bombs, or helping to drop them. It gets back to the old situation concerning combat fatigue.

The pros who carry nuclear arms today feel exactly the same moral responsibility they might feel in carrying a carbine or a 250-pound GP bomb. Or (I suppose there are pros among the Jivaros in South America, but maybe *they're* not yet armed with nuclear weapons) a poisoned blow-gun dart.

There were absolutely no psychological repercussions in the attitude of our SAC personnel after they became equipped with these weapons. I never observed any reluctance among my subordinates to embrace a program which entailed the employment of nuclear ordnance.

I can see no more reason for a delegation of Japanese maidens who were injured in Hiroshima or Nagasaki coming over here to protest against weapons, than I can for a throng of German civilians to demonstrate in front of the White House; or survivors of the attacks on Plymouth, London or Coventry to go over and stage a sit-down at the residence of the Chancellor of West Germany.

Certainly the feeling must be very much the same throughout all armies. From a practical standpoint of the soldiers out in the field it doesn't make any difference how you slay an enemy. Everybody worries about their own losses . . . seeing their friends killed, so on. As I've told before, I used to be tormented in losing my airmen . . . how many were shot down today? What could we have done instead? Was the prize worth the *price?* What could I have done which might have saved an extra crew or two . . . ?

But to worry about the *morality* of what we were doing—Nuts. A soldier has to fight. We fought. If we accomplished the job in any given battle without exterminating too many of our own folks, we considered that we'd had a pretty good day.

I can recognize no more depravity in dropping a nuclear weapon than in having a V-2 rocket equipped with an orthodox warhead, and shooting it vaguely in the general direction of London, as the Germans did. No difference whatsoever.

In fact, I think the preponderance of justice is on the side with a skillful weapon attacking a specific target. It must be remembered that we did not start the bombing in these wars. The Japs and the Germans did a lot of bombing before we ever got into the act.

. . . So some young kids who don't know any better go out and demonstrate against the military; and a lot of old fools who ought to know better, inveigh against the military, et cetera. They are worried to death about our dropping nuclear bombs.

In SAC our bombardiers aren't worried about it.

We were going after military targets. No point in slaughtering civilians for the mere sake of slaughter. Of course there is a pretty thin veneer in Japan, but the veneer was there. It was their system of dispersal of industry. All you had to do was visit one of those targets after we'd roasted it, and see the ruins of a multitude of tiny houses, with a drill press sticking up through the wreckage of every home. The entire population got into the act and worked to make those airplanes or munitions of war . . . men, women, children. We knew we were going to kill a lot of women and kids when we burned that town. Had to be done.

Oh, there was considerable dispersal of German industry, but never to the extent of the Japanese system. In Japan they were set up like this: they'd have a factory; and then the families, in their homes throughout the area, would manufacture small parts. You might call it a home-folks assembly line deal. The Suzuki clan would manufacture Bolt 64; the Harunobu family next door might be making Nut 64; or 65 or 63, or all the gaskets in between. Those would be manufactured right in the same neighborhood. Then Mr. Kitagawa from the factory would scoot around with his cart and pick up the parts in proper order.

I'll never forget Yokohama. That was what impressed me: drill presses. There they were, like a forest of scorched trees and stumps, growing up throughout that residential area. Flimsy construction all gone . . . everything burned down, or up, and drill presses standing like skeletons.

The whole purpose of strategic warfare is to destroy the enemy's potential to wage war. And this was the enemy's potential. It had to be erased. If we didn't obliterate it, we would dwell subservient to it. Just as simple as that.

. . . Did someone just say the word *co-existence?*

There's nothing new about this massacre of civilian populations. In ancient times, when an army laid siege to a city, everybody was in the fight. And when that city had fallen, and was sacked, just as often as not every single soul was murdered.

I think now of that elderly wheeze about the stupid man who was not basically cruel—he was just well-meaning. The guy who cut off the dog's tail an inch at a time so that it wouldn't hurt so much.

•   •   •

Certainly I did not and do not decry the use of the bomb. Anything which will achieve the desired results should be employed. If those bombs shortened the war only by days, they rendered an inestimable service, and so did the men who were responsible for their construction and delivery. There was no transgression, no venturing into a field illicit and immoral, as has so often been charged. Soldiers were ordered to do a job. They did it.

Questions

1. The voice behind this essay is distinctive. How would you describe this persona? Consider his descriptions of those who oppose nuclear warfare and of himself as "in the bombardment business." Give some thought to his response to the news of new ordnance ("Swell") and to his suggestion during the Korean War to "delete [with incendiary bombs] four or five of the largest towns" in North Korea. How do his word choices help to characterize him?

2. Do you agree with LeMay's contention that it is not "more wicked to kill people with a nuclear bomb, than to kill people by busting their heads with rocks"? Does his Biblical analogy work? Are there effective differences between the use of a nuclear bomb and a rock? Between a machine gun and a bow and arrow?

3. To what extent would a pacifist agree with LeMay? Where would he differ?

4. What arguments does LeMay use to justify the tactical use of nuclear weapons against Japan? Are his arguments cogent? What are their strengths and weaknesses?

Composition

1. If you disagree with LeMay on the use of atomic weapons in the Second World War, try to suggest an effective alternative to dropping the bombs on Hiroshima and Nagasaki. How could the United States have used the bombs without actually employing them against people?

2. If you agree with LeMay, write a letter to a bomb victim who survived, explaining why it was necessary to drop the bomb on his city. (For some responses of bomb victims see John Hersey's *Hiroshima*, Robert Jay Lifton's *Death in Life*, and Arata Osada's *Children of the A-Bomb*.)

3. War

To fight is a radical instinct; if men have nothing else to fight over they will fight over words, fancies, or women, or they will fight because they dislike each other's looks, or because they have met walking in opposite directions. To knock a thing down, especially if it is cocked at an arrogant angle, is a deep delight to the blood. To fight for a reason and in a calculating spirit is something your true warrior despises; even a coward might screw his courage up to such a reasonable conflict. The joy and glory of fighting lie in its pure spontaneity and consequent generosity; you are not fighting for gain, but for sport and for victory. Victory, no doubt, has its fruits for the victor. If fighting were not a possible means of livelihood the bellicose instinct could never have established itself in any long-lived race. A few men can live on plunder, just as there is room in the world for some beasts of prey; other men are reduced to living on industry, just as there are diligent bees, ants, and herbivorous kine. But victory need have no good fruits for the people whose army is victorious. That it sometimes does so is an ulterior and blessed circumstance hardly to be reckoned upon.

Since barbarism has its pleasures it naturally has its apologists. There are panegyrists of war who say that without a periodical

From *Little Essays* by George Santayana, Charles Scribner's Sons. Reprinted by permission of the publishers.

bleeding a race decays and loses its manhood. Experience is directly opposed to this shameless assertion. It is war that wastes a nation's wealth, chokes its industries, kills its flower, narrows its sympathies, condemns it to be governed by adventurers, and leaves the puny, deformed, and unmanly to breed the next generation. Internecine war, foreign and civil, brought about the greatest set-back which the life of reason has ever suffered; it exterminated the Greek and Italian aristocracies. Instead of being descended from heroes, modern nations are descended from slaves; and it is not their bodies only that show it. After a long peace, if the conditions of life are propitious, we observe a people's energies bursting their barriers; they become aggressive on the strength they have stored up in their remote and unchecked development. It is the unmutilated race, fresh from the struggle with nature (in which the best survive, while in war it is often the best that perish), that descends victoriously into the arena of nations and conquers disciplined armies at the first blow, becomes the military aristocracy of the next epoch and is itself ultimately sapped and decimated by luxury and battle, and merged at last into the ignoble conglomerate beneath. Then, perhaps, in some other virgin country a genuine humanity is again found, capable of victory because unbled by war. To call war the soil of courage and virtue is like calling debauchery the soil of love.

Blind courage is an animal virtue indispensable in a world full of dangers and evils where a certain insensibility and dash are requisite to skirt the precipice without vertigo. Such animal courage seems therefore beautiful rather than desperate or cruel, and being the lowest and most instinctive of virtues it is the one most widely and sincerely admired. In the form of steadiness under risks rationally taken, and perseverance so long as there is a chance of success, courage is a true virtue; but it ceases to be one when the love of danger, a useful passion when danger is unavoidable, begins to lead men into evils which it was unnecessary to face. Bravado, provocativeness, and a gambler's instinct, with a love of hitting hard for the sake of exercise, is a temper which ought already to be counted among the vices rather than the virtues of man. To delight in war is a merit in the soldier, a dangerous quality in the captain, and a positive crime in the statesman.

The panegyrist of war places himself on the lowest level on which a moralist or patriot can stand and shows as great a want of refined feeling as of right reason. For the glories of war are all blood-stained, delirious, and infected with crime; the combative instinct is a savage prompting by which one man's good is found in another's evil. The existence of such a contradiction in the moral world is the original sin of nature, whence flows every other wrong. He is a willing accomplice of that perversity in things who delights in another's discomfiture or in his own, and craves the blind tension of plunging into danger without reason, or the idiot's pleasure in facing a pure chance. To find joy in another's trouble is, as man is constituted, not unnatural, though it is wicked; and to find joy in one's own trouble, though it be madness, is not yet impossible for man. These are the chaotic depths of that dreaming nature out of which humanity has to grow.

Questions

1. In Santayana's view, is there ever a valid reason for war? What does he mean when he says: "The combative instinct is a savage prompting by which one man's good is found in another's evil"?

2. Santayana says: "To fight is a radical instinct." Do you agree? If so, do you see any hope that war can be abolished or, at least, controlled? Does Santayana have hope for the abolition or control of war?

3. Santayana stops short of suggesting concrete and specific ways by which man can begin to grow out of "the chaotic depths of that dreaming nature." Can you suggest any ways?

4. When is courage a virtue, when a vice? Can you find modern examples of these two aspects of courage?

Composition

1. Narrate a particular incident that illustrates and implicitly defines one or the other aspect of courage that Santayana discusses. Draw on your own experience. Make yourself a central figure or a witness. To put this assignment another way, you must try to make one of the two concepts of courage as concretely and vividly realizable as possible.

4. I Believe and Profess

CARL von CLAUSEWITZ

I believe and profess that a people never must value anything higher than the dignity and freedom of its existence; that it must defend these with the last drop of its blood; that it has no duty more sacred and can obey no law that is higher; that the shame of a cowardly submission can never be wiped out; that the poison of submission in the bloodstream of a people will be transmitted to its children, and paralyze and undermine the strength of later generations; that honor can be lost only once; that, under most circumstances, a people is unconquerable if it fights a spirited struggle for its liberty; that a bloody and honorable fight assures the rebirth of the people even if freedom were lost; and that such a struggle is the seed of life from which a new tree inevitably will blossom.

I declare and assert to the world and to future generations that I consider the false wisdom which aims at avoiding danger to be the most pernicious result of fear and anxiety. Danger must be countered with virile courage joined with calm and firm resolve and clear conscience. Should we be denied the opportunity of defending ourselves in this manner, I hold reckless despair to be a wise course of action. In the dizzy fear which is beclouding our days, I remain mindful of the ominous events of old and recent times, and of the honorable

From *War, Politics and Power* by Carl von Clausewitz, translated and edited by Edward M. Collins, Henry Regnery Co., A Gateway Edition, 1962, 1965.

examples set by famed peoples. The words of a mendacious newspaper do not make me forget the lessons of centuries and of world history.

I assert that I am free of all personal ambitions; that I profess thoughts and sentiments openly before all citizens; and that I would be happy to find a glorious end in the splendid battle for the freedom and excellence of my country.

Does my faith and the faith of those who think like me deserve the contempt and scorn of our citizens? Future generations will decide.

A nation cannot buy freedom from the slavery of alien rule by artifices and stratagems. It must throw itself recklessly into battle, it must pit a thousand lives against a thousand-fold gain of life. Only in this manner can the nation arise from the sick bed to which it was fastened by foreign chains.

Boldness, that noble virtue through which the human soul rises above the most menacing dangers, must be deemed to be a decisive agent in conflict. Indeed, in which sphere of human activity should boldness come into its own unless it be in struggle?

Boldness is the outstanding military quality, the genuine steel which gives to arms their luster and sharpness. It must imbue the force from camp follower and private to the commander-in-chief.

In our times, struggle, and, specifically, an audacious conduct of war are practically the only means to develop a people's spirit of daring. Only courageous leadership can counter the softness of spirit and the love of comfort which pull down commercial peoples enjoying rising living standards. Only if national character and habituation to conflict interact constantly upon each other can a nation hope to hold a firm position in the political world.

A nation which does not dare to talk boldly will risk even less to act with courage.

A nation does not go under because for one or two years it engages in efforts which it could not sustain for ten or twenty years. If the importance of the purpose demands it, and especially if it is a matter of maintaining independence and honor, such efforts are a call of duty. The government possesses all the means required to persuade the people to live up to their obligations. It is entitled to expect exertions, to insist on them, and if necessary is bound to compel compliance. Strong and purposive governments, which are truly capable of managing affairs, never will fail to act in this manner.

Perhaps there never again will be times when nations will be obliged to take refuge in the last desperate means of popular uprising against foreign domination. Yet in our epoch, every war inevitably is a matter of national interest and must be conducted in that spirit, with the intensity of effort which the strength of the national character allows and the government demands.

In my judgment the most important political rules are: never relax vigilance; expect nothing from the magnanimity of others; never abandon a purpose until it has become impossible, beyond doubt, to attain it; hold the honor of the state as sacred.

The time is yours; what its fulfillment will be, depends upon you. . . .

Questions

1.   How close is Clausewitz's "boldness" to Santayana's "bravado"?

2.   Writing in the early nineteenth century, Clausewitz does not tie his beliefs to anything more specific than "our time." Has his credo been applied more recently—in Vietnam, for instance, or in the First and Second World Wars? Applied to each of these wars, is his credo meaningful or outdated?

3.   Are Clausewitz's "most important political rules" still adhered to? By whom? Are there any groups within the United States today who follow Clausewitz's rules? Is their adherence wise? Is it just?

Composition

1.   Compare and contrast Clausewitz's view of war with Santayana's. Do they agree on anything; although perhaps with different emphases? Consider, as well, their attitudes toward the weakening of future generations. How does each believe that nations will be drained of their strength?

5. The Defense of Bataan and Corregidor

DOUGLAS MACARTHUR

On December 28th, I inaugurated guerrilla warfare in the central and southern group of islands. At this time, despite my pleas to Washington, supplies of food and weapons were running dangerously low. General Marshall had promised to expend every effort to insure that reinforcements would be sent, and it was upon this promise that I was able to sustain both the civilians and the military.

On January 10th, and again on January 17th, I wired Washington explaining the seriousness of the situation. We had been on half rations for some time now, and the result was becoming evident in the exhausted condition of the men. The limited area occupied by our forces did not offer any means of obtaining food, and we were therefore dependent upon communication by sea, the responsibility for which had passed out of my control. Since the blockade was lightly held, many medium-sized ships could have been loaded with supplies and dispatched along various routes. It seemed incredible to me that no effort was made to bring in supplies. I cannot over-emphasize the psychological reaction on the Filipinos. They were able to understand military failure, but the apparent disinterest on the part of the United States was incomprehensible. Aware of the efforts the Allies were making in Europe, their feelings ranged from bewilderment to revulsion.

From *Reminiscences,* by Douglas MacArthur, © 1964, Time, Inc.

No one will ever know how much could have been done to aid the Philippines if there had been a determined will-to-win. There was certainly an effort made by the War Department to obtain supply ships and crews. My old friend, Major Pat Hurley, now a brigadier general, was sent to Australia, and Colonel John A. Robenson to Java, but the results were negative. Only three cargo ships reached the Philippines, two at Cebu and one at Anakan, on the north coast of Mindanao.

The crux of the problem lay in the different interpretation given to local problems by Admiral Thomas C. Hart, the naval commander, and myself. He strongly advocated that all air missions be under his command when over water. His criticism of the air force was very sharp, especially after its defeat at Clark Field. Apparently, he was certain that the islands were doomed and made no effort to keep open our lines of supply. In addition to his refusal to risk his ships in resisting the landings made on Luzon, he made no effort to oppose the Japanese blockade. On Christmas Day, he withdrew the bulk of his forces to the Dutch East Indies, where his surface craft were largely destroyed in a series of hopeless naval actions. The naval wireless station on Corregidor, the experienced 4th Regiment of Marines, three gunboats, three minesweepers, six PT boats, and a few other craft, all under Admiral Rockwell, then passed to my command.

During this period, President Roosevelt expressed the debt owed the people of the Philippines for their fight against the aggressor, and pledged Allied efforts for the freedom and independence of the islands. On Corregidor, Manuel Quezon was sworn in for his second term as president of the commonwealth.

Since no significant naval effort was forthcoming, I regrouped my forces on Bataan into two corps. The North Luzon Force now became the I Corps under General Wainwright and occupied the left perimeter, and the II Corps, formerly the South Luzon Force under General Jones came under the command of General Parker, and held the right.

The 4th Marine Regiment, which was under the control of the Navy, was not committed to the heavy fighting on Bataan, being held in reserve for the actual defense of Corregidor, itself. Fighting became heavy along the entire front and the attacks by enemy bombers almost ceaseless. My anti-aircraft ammunition began to dwindle alarmingly, and I was forced to reduce this type of firing to little more than a token effort, with occasional bursts for purposes of deception. The water system and mains on Corregidor and our adjacent fortified islands were practically destroyed, and I had to institute rationing. It was apparent that the enemy was setting up a prepared attack in maximum strength.

On January 10th I received the following epistle:

To: General Douglas MacArthur
Commander-in-Chief
United States Army Forces in the Far East

Sir:
You are well aware that you are doomed. The end is near.
The question is how long you will be able to resist. You have already cut rations by half. I appreciate the fighting spirit of yourself and your troops who have been fighting with courage. Your prestige and honor have been upheld.

However, in order to avoid needless bloodshed and to save the remnants of your divisions and your auxiliary troops, you are advised to surrender.

In the meantime, we shall continue our offensive as I do not wish to give you time for defense. If you decide to comply with our advice, send a mission as soon as possible to our front lines. We shall then cease fire and negotiate an armistice. Failing that, our offensive will be continued with inexorable force which will bring upon you only disaster.

Hoping your wise counsel will so prevail that you will save the lives of your troops, I remain,

Yours very sincerely,
Commander-in-Chief,
The Japanese Expeditionary Force

When I failed to respond, they showered our lines with a leaflet reading:

The outcome of the present combat has been already decided and you are cornered to the doom. But, however, being unable to realize the present situation, blinded General MacArthur has stupidly refused our proposal and continues futile struggle at the cost of your precious lives.
Dear Filipino Soldiers!
There are still one way left for you. That is to give up all your

weapons at once and surrender to the Japanese force before it is
too late, then we shall fully protect you.

We repeat for the last!

Surrender at once and build your new Philippines for and by
Filipinos.

Every foxhole on Bataan rocked with ridicule that night.

My food situation had been increasingly prejudiced by the great number of civilians who had fled into Bataan with our army forces. The Japanese had craftily furthered this movement by driving the frightened population of the province of Zambales, just north of Bataan, into our lines, knowing full well we would feed them—a humanitarian measure which cut deeply into our food stocks. I had to establish refugee camps back of our defense positions for many thousands of these forlorn people, mostly old men, women, and children. It forced me to cut the soldiers' ration not only in half, but later to one-quarter of the prescribed allowance. At the end we were subsisting on less than a thousand calories a day. Everywhere was that poignant prayer, "Give us this day our daily bread." The slow starvation was ultimately to produce an exhaustion which became the most potent factor in the destruction of the garrison.

Our headquarters, called "Topside," occupied the flattened summit of the highest hill on the island. It gave a perfect view of the whole panorama of the siege area. As always, I had to see the enemy or I could not fight him effectively. Reports, no matter how penetrating, have never been able to replace the picture shown to my eyes. The Filipinos, even as the smoke pillars of their burning villages dotted the land, were being told that Europe came first. Angry frustration, for citizens and soldiers alike, irritated bruised nerves and increased the sense of heartache and loss. And the enemy, night after night, in the seductive voice of "Tokyo Rose," rubbed raw the wounds by telling them over the radio that defeat and death were to be their fate while America's aid went elsewhere. President Quezon was stunned by the reports of the huge amounts of American supplies now being sent to Russia. His expression of bewildered anger was something I can never forget. As an evidence of assurance to these people suffering from deprivation, destruction, and despair, I deemed it advisable to locate headquarters as prominently as possible, notwithstanding exposure to enemy attack.

They came in a perfect formation of twin-engine bombers, glittering in the brilliant blue sky. Far-off, they looked like silver pieces thrown against the sun. But their currency was death and their appearance a deceit. These were deadly weapons of war and their bomb bays contained a terrible force of destruction. The long white main barracks, a concrete straight line, cracked and splintered like a glass box. The tin edges of the overhanging roof, under the impact of a thousand-pounder, were bent upward like the curvature of a Chinese pagoda. Pieces of the metal whirled through the air like bits of macabre confetti. A 500-pound burst took off the roof of my quarters. Telephone lines snapped and coiled to the ground. The sturdy rails and ties of the local streetcar line were loosed and looped up into meaningless form. The lawn became a gaping, smoking crater. Blue sky turned to dirty gray.

Then came strafing, and again the bombing. Always they followed the same pattern. Their own orders could not have enlightened me more. What I learned, I used to advantage later. They kept it up for three hours. The din was ferocious. The peaceful chirping of birds had been replaced by the shrill scream of dive bombers. The staccato of strafing was answered by the pounding of the anti-aircraft batteries. Machine guns chattered everywhere and ceaselessly. Then they left as shaking earth yielded under this pulverizing attack, and there rose a slow choking cover of dust and smoke and flame.

My new headquarters was located in an arm of the Malinta Tunnel. Carved deep in the rock, the central tunnel was actually the terminal point of a streetcar line. Other passages had been hewn out of the rock and these now housed hospital wards, storerooms, and ammunition magazines. The headquarters was bare, glaringly lighted, and contained only the essential furniture and equipment for administrative procedure. At the sound of the air alarm, an aide and I would make our way out through the crowded civilians seeking shelter in the main passageway, huddled silently in that hunched-down, age-old Oriental squat of patience and stolid resignation, onto the highway to watch the weaving pattern of the enemy's formations.

There was nothing of bravado in this. It was simply my duty. The gunners at the batteries, the men in the foxholes, they too were in the open. They liked to see me with them at such moments. The subtle corrosion of panic or fatigue, or the feeling of just being fed up, can only be arrested by the intervention of the leader. Leadership is often crystallized in some sort of public gesture. For example, in peace, such a gesture might be the breaking of bread as a symbol of hospitality, or with native Indians, the smoking of a peace pipe to show friendship. But in war, to be effective it must take the form of a fraternity of danger welded between a commander and his troops by the common denominator of sharing the risk of sudden death.

. . .

On January 12th, the Japanese struck in full force. In headlong attacks of unabated fury they tried to break the 20-mile peninsula de Fengo line from Abucay to Mauban. But our intimate knowledge of every inch of that bewildering area paid off. Our artillery, accurately placed in concealed positions for interdiction and flanking fire, completely stopped the bull-like rushes with such heavy slaughter as to leave their infantry, in spite of its great superiority in numbers, baffled and infuriated. They concentrated first on Abucay, our eastern anchor, and for a fleeting moment penetrated. But our counterattack promptly threw them out. They came again five days later, further to the west, but again failed. Again, three days later, in conjunction with a blind assault on Mauban, the western anchor of our line, they struck still further to the west. It was in vain. Attack and counterattack serrated the opposing lines in the bloodiest of hand-to-hand fighting.

Constantly, fresh Japanese troops arrived by transport to replace the enemy's losses. But I could only bury my dead. In all, nearly 100,000 replacements kept their original strength intact. At a critical moment, 150 guns of heavy caliber came in one shipment from Hong Kong. The pressure finally forced us to give ground. My men were beginning to feel the effects of malnutrition, and malaria was taking its toll of their vitality. They were unable to prevent the Japanese from infiltrating across the steep jungle-covered slopes of Mount Natib in the center of the defense line, and by the evening of January 25 General Wainwright had withdrawn from Mauban. We withdrew to our second line from Orion west to Bagac. They tried to storm this line, but were stopped in their tracks. By the end of January, General Homma had to temporarily cease major operations to await substantial reinforcements.

. . .

For the next six weeks the line successfully resisted all attempts at displacement. The enemy ceased his bloody frontal attacks, and Japanese records show that General Homma was on the point of giving up the effort to overwhelm us and substitute a plan to by-pass the islands, merely containing any war effort we might attempt. If only help could have reached the Philippines, even in small form, if only limited reinforcement could have been supplied, the end could not have failed to be a success. It was Japan's ability to continually bring in fresh forces and America's inability to do so that finally settled the issue.

. . .

Our troops were now approaching exhaustion. The guerrilla movement was going well, but on Bataan and Corregidor the clouds were growing darker. My heart ached as I saw my men slowly wasting away. Their clothes hung on them like tattered rags. Their bare feet stuck out in silent protest. Their long bedraggled hair framed gaunt bloodless faces. Their hoarse, wild laughter greeted the constant stream of obscene and ribald jokes issuing from their parched, dry throats. They cursed the enemy and in the same breath cursed and reviled the United States; they spat when they jeered at the Navy. But their eyes would light up and they would cheer when they saw my battered, and much reviled in America, "scrambled egg" cap. They would gather round and pat me on the back and "Mabuhay Macarsar" me. They would grin—that ghastly skeleton-like grin of the dying—as they would roar in unison, "We are the battling bastards of Bataan—no papa, no mama, no Uncle Sam."

They asked no quarter and they gave none. They died hard— those savage men—not gently like a stricken dove folding its wings in peaceful passing, but like a wounded wolf at bay, with lips curled back in sneering menace, and always a nerveless hand reaching for that long sharp machete knife which long ago they had substituted for the bayonet. And around their necks, as we buried them, would be a thread of dirty string with its dangling crucifix. They were filthy, and they were lousy, and they stank. And I loved them.

What happened here . . . ?—Official Marine Corps Photograph.

What happened here and what does it mean to those involved
(for example, to the living soldier, to the dead man, to his widow,
to the near-widow of the living man)? Write an imaginative account
of the events or their repercussions that this picture suggests to you.

Questions

1. Would MacArthur be more likely to agree with Santayana or Clausewitz?

2. How would you describe the tone of this narrative? What sort of man do you see writing this essay? What kind of audience do you think he has in mind? What is his relationship with his audience? Would you call it intimate, distant, or somewhere in between? How does he establish this relationship?

3. On what factors does MacArthur place much of the blame for the loss of Bataan and Corregidor? What evidence does he marshal? Is his evidence convincing?

4. Compare MacArthur's accounts of front-line deportment with those of Remarque, Douglas, and Chuikov, and those in the "Last Letters from Stalingrad." In each case, to what extent does the perspective of the author affect the interpretation of the situation?

Composition

1. The defense of Bataan and Corregidor would make an excellent research paper topic. Is there another side to the story MacArthur tells of his own good judgment and heroism? In addition to reading more fully in MacArthur's *Reminiscences,* see two books by Hanson W. Baldwin, *Great Mistakes of the War* and *Battles Won and Lost.* Other information may be found in Stanley L. Falk, *Bataan—The March of Death;* Samuel Eliot Morison, *The Rising Sun in the Pacific,* Vol. III of *History of U.S. Naval Operations in World War II;* and Jonathan Wainwright, *General Wainwright's Story.*

Part Four

STALINGRAD

"Germany will be either a world power or will not be at all."

—ADOLF HITLER

1. The Stalingrad Cauldron

In the fall of 1942 German troops of the Sixth Army under the command of General Friedrich von Paulus entered the Russian city of Stalingrad. The Germans seemed irresistable and believed themselves to be so, but they had underestimated badly the depth of Russian resources, the patient will of the Russian army, the immense logistical problem of thousand-mile-long supply lines, and the incredible severity of the Russian winter which had undone Napoleon more than a century before and which settled on the Germans after their attack stalled. Swiftly and suddenly, the initiative fell to the Russians. The Sixth Army was surrounded and cut off from their comrades in the south. The obvious need to break out of what became known as the Stalingrad Cauldron was delayed by Hitler's refusal to retreat and give up the historic Russian city. His orders to hold were relaxed far too late. An army of nearly 200,000 men was lost, and the war in the east had seen its climax.

The following selections are about the Battle of Stalingrad. Each writer sees it from a different perspective.

EXTRACTS FROM THE WAR DIARY OF AIR FLEET FOUR AND THE PERSONAL DIARY OF GENERAL VON RICHTHOFEN, COMMANDER OF AIR FLEET FOUR

12 *December* 1942. Good, clear weather. At 0430 hours Fourth Panzer Army's attack under General Hoth got off to a smooth start. Air force units are co-operating. . . .

v. R(ichthofen) had a conference with v. Manstein. Subject: lack of co-operation and the general situation. v. R(ichthofen) regards the situation as critical. He is urging Zeitzler to reinforce the army and to give us back the air formations which have been seconded from us. Expressed his views very forcibly to Jeschonnek over the telephone and said: "My faith in our leadership is rapidly sinking to zero."

13 *December*. Many fog patches, strong wind. v. R(ichthofen) to Semichmaya, where Fourth Panzer Army and LVII Panzer Corps are attacking. Divisions, he says, are all attacking too late, because they wait for a Russian counter-attack that never comes. "Of any real attempt to pour forward, to press on towards Stalingrad—not a trace! Here they're all shilly-shallying about against enemy forces that are known to be weak. The GOC (i.e. General Kirchner, commanding LVII Panzer Corps) has only a very sketchy idea of how precarious the situation at Stalingrad is; but in any case, his heart is not in the job."

14 *December*. Very bad weather, misty, fine rain, warm. Except for small air-lift to Stalingrad (80 tons fuel), no flying possible.

15 *December*. Ground fog. Air reconnaissance and intervention in land battle both impossible. We managed nevertheless to fly 70 tons into Stalingrad. Russians are attacking Fourth Panzer Army from every direction and are throwing our people back on to the Aksay. There's nothing we can do to help. Sixth Army's chances are becoming slimmer and slimmer.

16 *December*. v. R(ichthofen) notes: Today 27 and 51 Bomber Squadrons were taken away from us. This means that tomorrow's

---

From *Paulus and Stalingrad* by Walter Goerlitz, Citadel Press, 1963 © Bernard and Graefe, Verlag für Wehrwesen, Frankfurt am Main 1960.

attack will be robbed of a third of its air support. That we should get as far as the Aksay was obvious from the start, since up to that point the Russians have nothing but outposts. It was in the area immediately beyond the river that the battle began in earnest, and it is from this area that our troops are now being thrown out.

Tomorrow's attack goes in against an enemy who has proved his superiority. That it will succeed in achieving a real breakthrough is more than doubtful. Further to reduce its striking power by robbing it of one third of its air support means that we are abandoning Sixth Army to its fate—and that is plain murder. I said as much to Jeschonnek and formally disclaimed all responsibility. Deluding himself with stupid arguments, he won't believe me. He insists that, with the Italians scattered to the four winds, Sixth Army couldn't be rescued anyway. Tried to prove to me that I myself had consistently drawn attention to the importance of this sector of the front and had always advocated that it should be strengthened. But he forgets not only that I was always of the opinion—and still am—that Sixth Army ought to be withdrawn from the Volga and got out of the cauldron, but also that I had insisted that to continue to support the Italians, once our relief operations had started, would be impossible. I told v. Manstein all this. We both feel the same—that we're like a couple of attendants in a lunatic asylum! . . .

17 *December.* A sudden sharp frost. Tanks can now get a move on. v. R(ichthofen) again touring round, but, as he puts it, "Devoid of any optimism. We must just blunder on and do our duty." Bad news from the Italian sector. Two divisions have broken and fled in panic.

18 *December.* Despairing telegrams from Sixth Army to Air Fleet regarding food situation. These have been sent on to Air Force Headquarters. . . .
". . . In the evening a long discussion with v. Manstein on the subject of Sixth Army fighting its way out. To fly in the volume of stores demanded just can't be done. We had a heart-to-heart talk about the lack of drive in the conduct of operations and the general situation. v. Manstein told me that a report is being submitted to Hitler this evening, recommending that Sixth Army be ordered to fight its way out. He seemed to regard Hitler's agreement as a foregone conclusion."

19 *December.* v. Manstein today ordered Sixth Army to break-out

south-westwards . . . 154 aircraft carried 289 tons of supplies to Stalingrad. . . .

". . . But now the Fuehrer has ordered that Stalingrad will be held" [notes v. R(ichthofen)]. "In this connection, I learned from v. Manstein and Zeitzler that at the final conference on the subject the Reichsmarshal had expressed the view that the supply situation wasn't nearly as bad as it was made out to be. Apart from the fact that it would do his figure a power of good to spend a little time in the cauldron, I can only assume that my reports are either not read or are given no credence. In the old days, one could have done something about it, but nowadays one is treated like a silly kid and has no say at all!'"

STALINGRAD IN RETROSPECT *by Field-Marshal Friedrich Paulus*

The whole of the Stalingrad complex consists of three phases:

(1) The Drive to the Volga.
Within the framework of the war as a whole, the 1942 summer offensive represented an attempt to achieve by further offensive action what we had failed to achieve in the late autumn of 1941—namely, to bring the eastern campaign to a swift and victorious conclusion— which, after all, was one of the primary objects of the sudden onslaught on Russia—in the expectation that this would lead to our winning the whole war.

In the minds of the military commanders, it was this purely military aspect that was predominant. This basic attitude regarding Germany's last chance of winning the war dominated all our military thinking during the two phases ahead.

(2) With the launching of the Russian November offensive and the encirclement of the Sixth Army and part of the Fourth Panzer Army

---

From *Paulus and Stalingrad* by Walter Goerlitz, Citadel Press, 1963 © Bernard and Graefe, Verlag für Wehrwesen, Frankfurt am Main 1960.

—some 220,000 men in all—the emphasis shifted from "the victorious conclusion of the Russian campaign" to the question: how can we avoid being completely defeated in the east and thus losing the whole war?

It was this latter that was uppermost in the minds of both the commanders and the rank and file of Sixth Army, while higher authority—Army Group, Army and Supreme Headquarters—still believed, or at least pretended to believe, that we still had a chance of ultimate victory.

As a result, there arose a sharp divergence of opinion regarding plans for the further conduct of operations and the methods to be employed to implement them. Since higher authority, adhering still to the more optimistic appreciation mentioned above and promising immediate support, had forbidden Sixth Army to try to fight its way out during the first phase of the battle of encirclement (when it could quite easily have done so), the Army subsequently had no alternative but to stand and fight. Any other, independent action on its part might well have led to complete disorganization and the subsequent dissolution of the whole of the southern sector of the eastern theatre of war. Had that happened, not only would all hope of ultimate victory have been irremediably destroyed but very swiftly all possibility of avoiding decisive defeat and the consequent collapse of the whole eastern front would have disappeared.

(3) In the third phase, after the attempt to relieve Sixth Army had foundered and the promised help had failed to materialize, our sole objective was to gain time and thus to make possible the creation of a new front in the southern sector and the rescue of the very strong German forces operating in the Caucasus.

If we did not succeed in this, then the magnitude of our defeat in the eastern theatre would alone have sufficed to ensure our losing the whole war.

By this time, the higher authorities themselves had also adopted the line that we must "hold out at all costs," if the worst were to be avoided. The question of the resistance to be offered by the Sixth Army culminated therefore in the following problem: As I myself saw the situation and, even more, as the situation was depicted to me by those above, total defeat could be avoided only if Sixth Army fought on to the very last. All the more recent wireless signals were couched in the same sense—"every additional hour counts" and

Preparation Official U.S. Air Force Photography.

Readiness Wide World Photos.

(repeatedly from the neighbors on our right) "How much longer can Sixth Army hang on?"

From the time the cauldron was formed, and more particularly after the failure of Fourth Panzer Army's attempt to relieve us at the end of December, I, as the Army Commander, was confronted with violently conflicting considerations.

On the one hand were the stream of strict orders to hold fast, the repeated promises of help and admonitions of increasing urgency that I must be guided by the situation as a whole. On the other hand there was the purely human aspect of the increasing and incredible hardships and suffering which my troops were being called upon to endure and which inevitably caused me to ask myself whether the time had not come for me to give up the struggle.

But, deeply though I sympathized with the troops committed to my care, I still believed that the views of higher authority must take precedence; that Sixth Army must accept its agony, must make all

The Rest Wide World Photos.

the sacrifices demanded of it, if by so doing, we would ensure—as they themselves were convinced we should—that the even greater number of their comrades in neighboring armies would be rescued and saved.

I believed that by prolonging to its utmost our resistance in Stalingrad I was serving the best interests of the German people, for, if the eastern theatre of war collapsed, I saw no possible prospect of a peace by political negotiation.

To have stepped on my own responsibility out of the general framework, to have acted deliberately against the orders given to me would have entailed the acceptance of a sequence of responsibilities: at the outset, by breaking out, I should have been responsible for the fate of my neighbors; later, by prematurely giving up the fight, for that of the southern sector and with it the whole of the eastern front; and that would have meant—or so at least it seemed—that I should have been responsible to the German people for the loss of the whole war. In that case they would not have hesitated to place on me the whole blame for everything that had happened in the eastern theatre.

And (with the future outcome still hidden from us) what convincing and valid arguments could the Commander of the Sixth Army have produced in support of his disobedience of orders in the presence of the enemy?

Does the fact that his troops are in a position that is hopeless, or threatens to become so, give a Commander the right to refuse to obey orders? In the case of Stalingrad, it could by no means be asserted with certainty that our position was hopeless or even—except at the very end—that it threatened to become so. How, then, could I later have demanded obedience, or even felt justified in doing so, from one of my subordinates in a situation of, in his opinion, similar danger?

Does the prospect of his own death or the probable destruction or capture of his troops release the Commander from his soldierly duty to obey orders?

That is a question which each individual must today leave to his own conscience to answer.

At the time of which I am writing, neither the nation nor the Armed Forces would have understood my acting in this manner. It would have been an unequivocal, revolutionary, political act against Hitler. Furthermore, it is at least possible that, by abandoning Stalingrad contrary to orders, I should have been playing into Hitler's hands and given him the opportunity of castigating the cowardice and disobedience of his generals and putting upon them the whole blame for the military defeat that was looming larger and larger.

I should, too, have prepared the ground for a new myth, that of the Stalingrad stab in the back, to the great detriment of the German people's ability to form an accurate picture of the history of this war and to draw the conclusions that it is so important that they should draw.

The possibility of initiating a *coup d'état,* of deliberately inviting defeat, in order to bring about the downfall of Hitler and his National-Socialist régime as obstructions to the ending of the war never entered into my deliberations, nor, so far as I am aware, was any such idea ever mooted by anyone anywhere within the limits of my command.

Such ideas not only played no part in my deliberations, but would also have been wholly out of keeping with my character and outlook. I was a soldier, and I believed that it was by obeying orders that I could best serve my people.

As regards the responsibility of my subordinate commanders, they, tactically speaking, were under the same compulsion to obey my orders as I myself was, in the broader sphere, to carry out the strategic conceptions imposed upon me.

The responsibility—*vis à vis* the officers and men of the Sixth Army and the German people—for having obeyed orders and resisted till we could do no more and collapsed is mine and mine alone.

HITLER'S ORDER TO HOLD—*The Testimony of Friedrich Paulus at the Nuremberg War Trials, Feb. 12, 1946*

About 20 January, as I said, I had made a report that conditions had reached such a measure of misery and of suffering through cold, hunger, and epidemics as to be unbearable, and that to continue the fighting would be beyond human possibility. The answer given to me by the Supreme Command was:

"Capitulation is impossible. The 6th Army will do its historic duty by fighting to the utmost, in order to make the reconstruction of the Eastern front possible."

Questions

1.   Von Richthofen describes the attempt by German forces in the south to break through to their comrades surrounded at Stalingrad. Why does he give the rescue attempt little chance of success? Why does he say that he and von Manstein feel "like a couple of attendants in a lunatic asylum"?

2.   Both in his retrospective and his testimony at the Nuremberg war trials, Paulus blames the German high command and Hitler for the loss of so many men at Stalingrad. Does von Richthofen's record support Paulus? What argument does Paulus offer to justify fighting on after the situation had become hopeless? Is his argument convincing?

3.   What is the "new myth" that Paulus refers to in the paragraph beginning: "I should, too, have prepared the ground for a new myth . . ."? What are the conclusions that he feels are important for the German people to draw?

Composition

1.   A research paper on the Battle of Stalingrad could be exciting and rewarding. Many historians believe that the Germans had the military capability to defeat the Russians in this battle. What decisions led to the German defeat at Stalingrad? There are many good books on the subject including Walter Goerlitz, *Paulus and Stalingrad;* Vasili I. Chuikov, *The Battle for Stalingrad;* Alan Bullock, *Hitler, A Study in Tyranny* (2nd ed.) ; Paul Carell, *Hitler Moves East;* Erich von Manstein, *Lost Victories;* and Hanson W. Baldwin, *Battles Lost and Won.*

2.   Several members of the class might work together to produce on audio tape an aural documentary on the Battle of Stalingrad. A narrative voice could tie together dramatic renditions of various points of view, including some of those printed in this book. Careful selection and judicious use of music and other sound effects could make this composition a powerful statement about war.

2. Snowball

VASILI I. CHUIKOV

Many reconnaissance parties operated heroically during the October fighting. One of them, affectionately called "Snowball," was known up and down the front. It derived its name from the surname of its commander, Sergeant, afterwards Lieutenant, Snegov.[1] There were seven men in the party, but normally three or five men went out on reconnaissance at any one time, the remainder waited for their comrades to return, and rested in readiness to go out themselves on some dangerous mission, often involving the most unexpected adventures.

This remarkable group operated almost always surely and successfully. It was highly elusive. The men in it could escape notice even when it would have seemed impossible to remain hidden from the enemy's sharp-eyed observers.

When the small parties set off they were normally given instructions to make observations, and avoid any skirmishes with the enemy.

The men in the "Snowball" group were distinguished by their exceptional courage, and on their return from their missions often brought in prisoners for interrogation, or raided enemy headquarters and stores.

From *The Battle for Stalingrad* by Marshal Vasili Chuikov. Translated by Harold Silver. Copyright © by MacGibbon and Kee, Ltd. Reprinted by permission of Holt, Rinehart, and Winston, Inc.

[1] From the Russian "sneg": meaning snow.

On 8 October 1942, the reconnaissance party was given the job of getting through to the vicinity of Vishnevaya Gully, and finding out what enemy forces were being concentrated there. This was not the easiest of jobs. The group was under Snegov himself. He had three other men with him—Koryakin, Gryzlov and Abel. Their weapons consisted of three tommy-guns, twelve hand-grenades and a small-bore rifle. Apart from weapons, the group took radio equipment, telephone apparatus, rations and medical supplies. They were to set off early that day from the bank of the Volga, heading behind the enemy lines through Banny Gully. They went as far as the main road from the tractor factory southward to the centre of the city, and here they stopped.

"Let's watch the enemy's movements till nightfall," Snegov told the others. "We'll listen, watch and remember everything that will help us to go on further."

Dusk fell, followed by the darkness of an October evening. Two more hours passed. By scarcely distinguishable sounds. Snegov realized that under cover of darkness some Germans were going back into the rear.

"It looks as though they've gone for dinner. Well, let's wish them a good appetite," said the commander jestingly. "And now, my friends, off we go!"

And the group set off along the bottom of the gully towards the railway bridge, about five hundred yards south of the Krasny Oktyabr settlement.

To cover this distance, speed was needed, but speed of a special kind. Pressing themselves close to the ground they had to crawl over a mile, literally alongside the enemy. Snegov went ahead, followed by the others, ready to obey his command at any given moment. It took the group about an hour and a half to reach the railway bridge across Banny Gully. Then, finally, there was the railway line. The slightest careless movement, and all was lost. But Snegov and his men had their wits about them.

Snegov gestured to the men to take cover. The group rapidly occupied a position by the railway line, where they could not be seen, but could see what was going on around them. As if sensing the danger the Germans sent up rockets from the top of Mamayev Kurgan and from the Krasny Oktyabr settlement. The Germans were clearly losing their nerve. But the Germans could not see anything. By the light of the rockets, however, the reconnaissance group examined the shattered trucks and engines on the railway tracks. This conglomeration of wood and metal stretched almost in a continuous line north-westward to the Krasny Oktyabr settlement. They were quick to realize that it would be possible to establish an excellent observation post in the shattered trucks, and use them as a shelter for the whole group.

"The Germans surely can't start examining every broken-down truck and engine along the whole of this enormous cemetery of metal," thought Snegov, and whispered his decision to the others.

"After me!" He gave the command almost soundlessly and crawled along the railway track.

From time to time Snegov stopped, listened to the slightest rustle, and, when he was sure that there was no danger, crawled on again. Crawling on like this for about a mile, the group reached the southern outskirts of the Krasny Oktyabr settlement. But when the men started to approach the railway trucks the Germans again sent up rockets. The night sky became more and more alive with flares and aeroplanes. But all went well. The Germans did not see the reconnaissance group, which, by the light of the enemy rockets, was able to choose one of the metal trucks which was less buckled than the others. It was apparently a truck that had carried coal. Another goods waggon was piled up on top of it. Such a "two-storey detached residence" would serve as a good observation post. With great care they climbed up to the "second storey" and decided to rest till morning.

At dawn they took precise bearings of the co-ordinates of the observation post: they were half a mile east of Vishnevaya Gully, and where they needed to be to carry out their mission. They had a reliable shelter, which enabled them to observe the locality for a long way round. To the north of the observation post, some three hundred yards away, was the Krasny Oktyabr settlement. Half a mile or so to the north-west was Hill 107.5. West of the post were orchards, and to the south-east, on Mamayev Kurgan, were the two water-tanks.

The co-ordinates could now be sent by radio to H.Q., together with a report of what had been done, and observations could continue.

From daybreak they could hear the drone of enemy aircraft overhead. At the beginning they were single reconnaissance planes, followed later by bombers, carrying their load of death to the city, to its factories, houses and the positions occupied by the defenders. Almost simultaneously the enemy opened fire with artillery and mortars. In reply, shells and mortar bombs dropped on the enemy not far away, from the direction of the Volga. But where were the Germans firing from? The reconnaissance men soon detected dozens of enemy artillery and mortar batteries posted in the area west of Hill 107.5 and the Krasny Oktyabr settlement. Continuing their observation, they detected movement along the road from Gorodishche, in the region of Gumrak. It appeared to be columns of enemy artillery and mortars. Reaching the afforestation area bordering on the city to the west, they were beginning to take up firing positions. Following the guns came lorries, which began unloading what was presumably boxes of ammunition alongside the guns.

It was difficult to see exactly what all this meant. But they understood that fresh enemy forces were arriving on this sector of the front, and that the enemy was presumably preparing for a strong attack from this area. A report on what they had seen needed to be sent quickly by radio. Using the transmitter was no easy matter, as it might be detected by the enemy, particularly as the reconnaissance party's observation post was right inside the enemy positions.

The information they sent in was of great value to Army H.Q. What was needed now was to know what units the enemy had in the area of Vishnevaya Gully. To find this out a prisoner was needed. The "Snowball" party was instructed to get one.

On the same day, at 4 p.m., they reported to H.Q.:

"On Hill 107.5 there are a lot of observation posts, and telephone lines are being laid; north of the railway line, in the vicinity of Vishnevaya Gully, there is a build-up of artillery and ammunition taking place. Our task is clear, and tomorrow morning we will study the situation in the area of Vishnevaya Gully."

During the daytime they observed the enemy without binoculars. German soldiers, alone and in groups, were passing up and down the road from the Krasny Oktyabr settlement alongside the orchards. They had no thought for any danger that might be lurking. On the western outskirts of the Krasny Oktyabr settlement smoke was rising from field kitchens. Soldiers gathered round the water-hydrant, gossiping leisurely as they collected water. Between the reconnaissance group's observation post and the settlement, German signallers were laying a cable along the ground from the west towards Hill 107.5. Shells burst here and there, "presents" from our artillery . . . .

After discussing with the others the best way of capturing a prisoner, the commander of the group decided to organize an ambush along the road between the Krasny Oktyabr settlement and the orchards, and take a prisoner in the evening. If they failed to take one alive, then they would use the German's documents to get among the crowd of enemy soldiers by the kitchens and water-hydrant, and also listen in on the telephone line to what the Germans were talking about.

The most difficult part of the operation was taking the prisoner. The job was going to be done by Snegov, Koryakin, an experienced scout, and Abel, who spoke fluent German. Gryzlov, the radio operator, was to continue his observations and send in radio reports. The three men took their telephone apparatus with them, and also the small-bore rifle, a tommy-gun, daggers and hand grenades. Abel, in addition, had a policeman's rubber truncheon, captured on one of their previous missions.

When darkness fell, the three of them left the truck and set off towards the railway crossing south of the Krasny Oktyabr settlement. Finding the telephone line, they set about tapping it. They then carefully moved the cable ten or so yards to the side of the road, into the bushes, and cut it. Snegov and Koryakin then moved off in different directions to wait for the German telephonists who would come looking for the break in the line. Abel stayed by the cable. A German signaller soon appeared from the direction of the orchards, flashing a torch on the cable, looking for the break. The torch-light worried our men, because they might be seen by it. Snegov took a quick decision. Koryakin and Abel hid in the bushes and waited until the German signaller came up to the point where they had cut the cable. Snegov hid some distance away. When the German came up close and switched on the torch to examine the cable, there was a click from the breech of the rifle in Koryakin's hands, and the German fell. Abel leaped from behind the bushes with the rubber truncheon ready, but the German showed no signs of life. They dragged the dead German into the bushes, and Abel emerged dressed as a German soldier, with documents in the name of Hans Müller. Leaving Koryakin on watch, Snegov and Abel listened in at the end of the line from the Krasny Oktyabr direction. They could hear a rustling sound in the receiver, and then a call. Abel answered the call in German, asking:

"Who's on line duty?"

"Willi, one of our telephonists. Who's coming to meet him?"

"I am, Hans," answered Abel. "I've found the break. But there's not enough cable to join the ends. Send a few yards with Willi."

"Right," came the answer.

At the end of the conversation "Hans" asked for Willi to come as soon as possible to the railway line.

"I'll meet him there," said Abel.

And Abel went towards the railway line and stood at the top of the slope, so that he could be seen from a distance; five yards from Abel, with the small-bore rifle, Snegov lay hidden.

Soon they heard steps, and then they made out an approaching silhouette. This was presumably Willi. He crossed the railway line and started to climb up the steep slope. "Hans" shone his torch on him and stretched out his hand to help him to the top. When the signaller gave him his hand, Abel gripped it hard and brought the rubber truncheon down hard on the man's head . . .

After gagging the unconscious German, the two men dragged him to the railway trucks. Then, together with Koryakin, they joined the broken ends of the cable and repaired the line. This would re-assure whoever had sent the signallers to repair the damage, so that they would not send anyone else. Leaving Koryakin to keep a look out, Snegov told Gryzlov to get the transmitter ready to send a report. The prisoner had by now come to, and the interrogation could begin.

But how were they going to interrogate him? What if he suddenly yelled out?

"Ask him questions, and let him answer them on paper. We're not taking his gag off," ordered Snegov.

Abel translated Snegov's instructions, and so that the German could write, they freed his right hand, and gave him a pencil and paper. The decision was a very sensible one. By answering the questions in writing, the German could not cry out and attract the attention of his compatriots, and at the same time our men obtained an important document. The German would now hardly do anything that would lead to the capture of our men with this document in their possession.

"Your Christian name, surname, unit and where you are posted?" Abel asked the prisoner.

"Willi Brandt, of the 274th Regiment," wrote the prisoner.

The prisoner stopped answering questions, and begged for water. The reconnaissance men had no choice but to try to satisfy his request. Unfortunately, they had no water left. What were they going to do? Taking two billy-cans, and taking advantage of the darkness, Abel strode off towards the Krasny Oktyabr settlement for water. He walked confidently through the settlement, answering the greetings of German soldiers he met. On the western outskirts of the settlement he even thought of going up to a group of soldiers waiting for their evening meal, so as to listen to what they were talking about, but he resisted the temptation. As soon as he had got some water he returned to his comrades.

When the prisoner's gag was taken off and he could speak, he gave not only his name and regiment, but his unit and where he was posted. After he had drunk a few mouthfuls he was ready to give more information.

He told them that the 274th Infantry Regiment was being incorporated into the 94th Infantry Division, which had arrived here from the vicinity of Sadovaya Station and Minina suburb at the beginning of October. He also told them that, as a signaller, he had recently listened to a telephone conversation between officers of regimental H.Q. From this conversation he had gathered that the 24th Panzer Division, with more than a hundred and fifty tanks, had arrived, that units of a light infantry division had been sent to the Krasny Oktyabr settlement, that Hitler had demanded that the city be occupied by October 15, and that preparations were therefore going ahead for a decisive offensive.

The veracity of what Willi Brandt had told them was confirmed by the information that they had already gleaned.

"You have betrayed a military secret," Snegov told the prisoner. "And if your regiment finds out, you will be shot."

The German was now not overjoyed at the idea of returning to his unit, and his expression showed the fact.

"Don't be afraid," Abel reassured him. "We are not going to give you away. But you are not to tell a soul what has happened, and at every available opportunity you should tell your mates that the Russians don't shoot their prisoners and that German soldiers don't need to be afraid of captivity, and the main thing is that they ought not to fight against the Soviet people."

The prisoner listened to him, then asked:

"And how am I going to explain the bump on my head and my long absence? It's a long time since I was sent out on the line . . ."

They told him how to get out of his difficulty:

"Tell them you fell down the railway embankment and knocked yourself unconscious."

He cheered up a bit.

They then led him to the spot where they had taken him prisoner, gave him some telephone cable, and showed him how to get back to Hill 107.5.

Continuing to look mistrustfully at the rifle. Willi Brandt started down the slope. When he was sure that he was safe, he waved his hand and said: *"Danke, Kamerad,"* did not look back any more, and set off along the path they had shown him.

Questions

1.   Chuikov was the commander of the Russian Sixty-second Army at Stalingrad. The heroes in victory that he describes seem very much like MacArthur's heroes in defeat. Neither of these groups resembles Remarque's or Douglas's soldiers. Can you tell from considering all of these views together what front-line warfare is really like? To what extent does the speaker's identity affect his attitude in each case?

2.   In the second of the Stalingrad letters printed in this section, the soldier writes to his antiwar friend: "It is so easy to say: Put down your weapons. Do you think the Russians will spare us?" In Chuikov's account, the Russian soldier Abel says to Willi his prisoner: "At every available opportunity you should tell your mates that the Russians don't shoot their prisoners and that German soldiers don't need to be afraid of captivity." Where does the truth lie?

3.   Is Chuikov's version of the reconnaissance mission completely credible? Several acts of bravery are performed on the venture. Does any of them sound manipulated or contrived? Has any detail been left out of the story Willi is given to explain his injury and long absence? Is his farewell response believable?

4.   What moves men in war to volunteer for dangerous assignments like the one described here?

Composition

1.   Rewrite a portion of this section to remove the weight of post-war Soviet propaganda and to increase credibility. Try, perhaps to recreate the capture, interrogation, and release of Willi Brandt, writing either from Willi's point of view or from that of one of the Russian soldiers.

2.   Write a narrative account of the most dangerous thing that you have ever done.

3. Last Letters from Stalingrad

These letters were written by soldiers who knew that their situation was bad or hopeless. They were told that one last mail plane would leave Stalingrad and that these letters might be the last they could get out. The letters were flown out, but they were not delivered. Instead, when they arrived in Germany they were confiscated by the Bureau of Army Information for a study of troop morale. At first, they were destined for publication by the army as documents of German valor at Stalingrad. Their contents, however, appalled the analysts, and the letters were suppressed. Authenticated copies of them were found in the army archives in Potsdam after the war.

I

. . . You must get that out of your head, Margaret, and you must do do it soon. I would even advise you to be ruthless about it, for your disappointment will be less. In every one of your letters I sense your desire to have me home with you soon. It isn't strange at all that you

From *Last Letters from Stalingrad*, translated by Franz Schneider and Charles Gullans. Reprinted by permission of William Morrow and Company, Inc. Copyright © 1961 by The Hudson Review, Inc.

are looking forward to it. I too am waiting and longing for you passionately. That is not so much what disturbs me, but rather the unspoken desire I read between your lines to have not only the husband and lover with you again, but also the pianist. I feel that very distinctly. Is it not a strange confusion of feeling that I, who should be most unhappy, have resigned myself to my fate, and the woman who should have every reason to be thankful that I am still alive (at least so far) is quarreling with the fate that has struck me?

At times I have the suspicion that I am being silently reproached, as if it were my fault that I can play no longer. That's what you wanted to hear. And that's why you kept probing in your letters for the truth which I would have much preferred to tell you in person. Perhaps it is the will of destiny that our situation here has come to a point which permits no excuses and no way out. I do not know whether I shall have a chance to talk to you once more. So it is well that this letter should reach you, and that you know, in case I should turn up some day, that my hands are ruined and have been since the beginning of December. I lost the little finger on my left hand, but worse still is the loss of the three middle fingers of my right hand through frostbite. I can hold my drinking cup only with my thumb and little finger. I am quite helpless; only when one has lost his fingers does one notice how much they are needed for the simplest tasks. The thing I can still do best with my little finger is shoot. Yes, my hands are wrecked. I can't very well spend the rest of my life shooting, simply because I'm no good for anything else. Perhaps I could make out as a game warden? But this is gallows humor; I only write it to calm myself.

Kurt Hahnke, I think you remember him from the Conservatory in '37, played the Appassionata a week ago on a grand piano in a little side street close to Red Square. Such things don't happen every day. The grand piano was standing right in the middle of the street. The house had been blown up, but feeling sorry for the instrument, they must have got it out beforehand and put it in the street. Every passing soldier hammered away at it. I ask you, where else can you find a place with pianos in the streets? As I said, Kurt played incredibly well on January 4. He will be in the very front line soon.

Excuse me; here I am using the word "front line" instead of "first rank,"[1] such is the influence of war on us. If the boy gets home,

---

[1] The confusion is between *"vordersten Front"* and *"vordersten Reihe,"* the first of which refers to the line of combat and the second to artistic eminence.

we will soon hear about him. I certainly shall never forget these hours—the kind of audience and the situation were unique. Pity that I am not a writer, so that I could describe how a hundred soldiers squatted around in their great-coats with blankets over their heads. Everywhere there was the sound of explosions, but no one let himself be disturbed. They were listening to Beethoven in Stalingrad, even if they didn't understand him. Do you feel better now that you know the full truth?

II

. . . Just don't bother me with your well meant advice. Don't you know what kind of situation you'll get me into? The way you go on! You wouldn't have done it; you would have known how to do it! Things should have been done in such and such a way, etc., etc.! What is all that supposed to mean? You know that I am of your opinion and that we talked more about it than was safe. But you don't put that sort of thing in writing! Do you think the others are idiots?

If *I* write now, it is because I know that nothing can happen to me, and I took the precaution to leave off my name and return address; moreover, you will receive this letter in the agreed-on way. Even if anybody knew who wrote this letter, I couldn't be safer any place than in Stalingrad. It is so easy to say: Put down your weapons. Do you think the Russians will spare us? You are an intelligent man, so why don't you also demand that your friends refuse to produce ammunition and war materiel?

It is easy to give good advice; but it just won't work the way you think it will. Liberation of nations, nonsense. Nations remain the same. Their rulers change, and bystanders will keep arguing for liberating the people from their respective rulers. The time to act was in 1932; you know that very well. Also, that we let the moment go by. Ten years ago, the ballot would still have done the trick. To-day, all it will cost you is your life.

III

. . . You are my witness that I never wanted to go along with it, because I was afraid of the East, in fact of war in general. I have never been a soldier, only a man in uniform. What do I get out of it? What do the others get out of it, those who went along and were not afraid? Yes, what are we getting out of it? We, who are playing the walk-on parts in this madness incarnate? What good does a hero's death do us? I have played death on the stage dozens of times, but I was only playing, and you sat out front in plush seats, and thought my acting authentic and true. It is terrible to realize how little the acting had to do with real death.

You were supposed to die heroically, inspiringly, movingly, from inner conviction and for a great cause. But what is death in reality here? Here they croak, starve to death, freeze to death—it's nothing but a biological fact like eating and drinking. They drop like flies; nobody cares and nobody buries them. Without arms or legs and without eyes, with bellies torn open, they lie around everywhere. One should make a movie of it; it would make "the most beautiful death in the world" impossible once and for all. It is a death fit for beasts; later they will ennoble it on granite friezes showing "dying warriors" with their heads or arms in bandages.

Poems, novels, and hymns will be written and sung. And in the churches they will say masses. I'll have no part of it, because I have no desire to rot in a mass grave. I have written the same thing to Professor H—. You and he will hear from me again. Don't be surprised if it takes a while, because I have decided to take my fate into my own hands.

IV

. . . In Stalingrad, to put the question of God's existence means to deny it. I must tell you this, Father, and I feel doubly sorry for it. You have raised me, because I had no mother, and always kept God before my eyes and soul.

And I regret my words doubly, because they will be my last, and I won't be able to speak any other words afterwards which might reconcile you and make up for these.

You are a pastor, Father, and in one's last letter one says only what is true or what one believes might be true. I have searched for God in every crater, in every destroyed house, on every corner, in every friend, in my fox hole, and in the sky. God did not show Himself, even though my heart cried for Him. The houses were destroyed, the men as brave or as cowardly as myself, on earth there was hunger and murder, from the sky came bombs and fire, only God was not there. No, Father, there is no God. Again I write it and know that this is terrible and that I cannot make up for it ever. And if there should be a God, He is only with you in the hymnals and the prayers, in the pious sayings of the priests and pastors, in the ringing of the bells and the fragrance of incense, but not in Stalingrad.

V

. . . I have written to you twenty-six times from this damned city, and you answered me with seventeen letters. Now I shall write just once more and then never again. There, I said it. For a long time I thought about how I should formulate so fateful a sentence so that it would say everything and still not hurt too much.

I am saying good-bye to you, because since this morning the issue is settled. I will not comment on the military situation in my letter; it is clear-cut and completely up to the Russians. The only question is how long we will be around. It may last a few more days or just a few hours. Our whole life together is there for us to see. We have honored and loved each other, and waited for each other now for two years. It is good that so much time has passed. It has increased the anticipation of reunion, to be sure, but also in large measure helped to make us strangers. And time will have to heal the wounds of my not coming back.

In January you will be twenty-eight. That is still very young for such a good-looking woman, and I am glad that I could pay you this compliment again and again. You will miss me very much, but even so, don't withdraw from other people. Let a few months pass, but no more. Gertrud and Claus need a father. Don't forget that you must live for the children, and don't make too much fuss about their father. Children forget quickly, especially at that age. Take a good look at the man of your choice, take note of his eyes and the pressure of his handshake, as was the case with us, and you won't go wrong. But above all, raise the children to be upright human beings who can carry their heads high and look everybody straight in the eye. I am writing these lines with a heavy heart. You wouldn't believe me if I said that it was easy, but don't be worried, I am not afraid of what is coming. Keep telling yourself, and the children also when they have grown older, that their father never was a coward, and that they must never be cowards either.

VI

. . . I have received your answer. You will hardly expect thanks for it. This letter will be short. I should have known better when I asked you to help me. You always were and you remain forever "righteous." This wasn't unknown to either Mama or me. But we could hardly expect that you would sacrifice your son to "righteousness." I asked you to get me out of here because this strategic nonsense isn't worth biting the dust for. It would have been easy for you to put in a word for me, and the appropriate order would have reached me. But you don't understand the situation. Very well, Father.

This letter will not only be short, but also the last one I write you. I won't have any more opportunities to write to you, even if I wanted to. It is also unimaginable that I should ever stand face to face with you again and have to tell you what I think. And because neither I in person nor another letter will ever speak to you again, I will once more recall to you your words of December 26: "You became a soldier voluntarily; it was easy to stand under the flag in peacetime, but difficult to hold it high during the war. You will be faithful to this flag and be victorious with it." These words were much clearer than the position you have taken during the last few years. You will have to remember them, because the time is coming when every German with any sense will curse the madness of this war. And you will see how empty are those words about the flag with which I was supposed to be victorious.

There is no victory, Herr General; there are only flags and men that fall, and in the end there will be neither flags nor men. Stalingrad is not a military necessity but a political gamble. And your son is not participating in this experiment, Herr General! You blocked his way to life; he will choose the second way, which also leads to life, but in an opposite direction and on the other side of the front. Think of your words, and I hope that, when the whole show collapses, you will remember the flag and stand by it.

VII

. . . During the last few nights I have wept so much that it seems unbearable even to myself. I saw one of my fellow soldiers weep also, but for a different reason. He was weeping for the tanks he lost; they were his whole pride. And though I don't understand my own weakness, I do understand how a man can mourn dead war materiel. I am a soldier and I am prepared to believe that tanks are not inanimate materiel to him. But everything considered, the remarkable fact is that two men weep at all. I was always susceptible to tears. A moving experience or a noble action made me weep. It could happen in the movie theater, when I read a book, or saw an animal suffer. I cut myself off from external circumstances and immersed myself in what I saw and felt. But the loss of material goods never bothered me. Therefore, I would have been incapable of weeping about tanks which, when they ran out of gas, were used in the open steppes as artillery and thus easily shot to bits. But seeing a fine man, a brave, tough and unyielding soldier cry like a child over them—that did make my tears flow in the night.

On Tuesday I knocked out two T34s with my mobile anti-tank gun. Curiosity had lured them behind our lines. It was grand and impressive. Afterwards I drove past the smoking remains. From a hatch there hung a body, head down, his feet caught, and his legs burning up to his knees. The body was alive, the mouth moaning. He must have suffered terrible pain. And there was no possibility of freeing him. Even if there had been, he would have died after a few hours of torture. I shot him, and as I did it, the tears ran down my cheeks. Now I have been crying for three nights about a dead Russian tank driver, whose murderer I am. The crosses of Gumrak shake me and so do many other things which my comrades close their eyes to and set their jaws against. I am afraid I'll never be able to sleep quietly, assuming that I shall ever come back to you, dear ones. My life is a terrible contradiction, a psychological monstrosity.

I have now taken over a heavy anti-tank gun and organized eight men, four Russians among them. The nine of us drag the cannon from one place to another. Every time we change position, a burning tank remains on the field. The number has grown to eight already, and we intend to make it a dozen. However, I have only three rounds left, and shooting tanks is not like playing billiards. But during the night I cry without control, like a child. What will all this lead to?

Questions

1. "But, deeply though I sympathized with the troops committed to my care," says Paulus, "I still believed that the views of higher authority must take precedence . . . ." How would each of the writers of these letters respond to Paulus's argument for not surrendering early?

2. Try to describe the speaker in each of these letters. What was he like before the war? How has war changed him? In each case, to whom does he write? How much can you tell about his relationship with the addressee?

3. Consider letters IV and V. In these instances, is truth best?

4. What is death to the actor in letter III and to the gunner in letter VII? Why does the gunner cry every night? How do you explain his sudden change from feeling that knocking out tanks is "grand and impressive" to uncontrollable crying? Is he a murderer as he says? Why does he continue to fire on tanks?

5. Which letter would you choose as the most effective antiwar statement?

Composition

1. Each of the letters offers a skeletal situation about which much can be inferred. Suppose that these letters had been transmitted to you orally and that no written record exists of them but your notes. What would you write to the people addressed? Choose one letter and write to the person addressed (inventing a name), identifying yourself simply as someone who spoke to the writer just before Stalingrad fell. You have no knowledge of his fate, but feel obliged to convey his last thoughts to the addressee. Would you omit anything? Change anything? Add anything?

2. Suppose that you are the addressee of one of the letters and that you have received it. Compose a reply, assuming that the writer may still be alive. What would you say?

Part Five

VIETNAM

"It was no big deal."

—A G.I. TALKING ABOUT MY LAI

1. I Want the Killing to Stop

LYNDON BAINES JOHNSON

I do not genuinely believe that there's any single person anywhere in the world that wants peace as much as I want it. I want the killing to stop. I want us to join hands with others to do more in the fight against hunger and disease and ignorance. But we all know from hard-won experience that the road to peace is not the road of concession and retreat.

A lot of our friends tell us how troubled they are, and how frustrated they are. And we are troubled. And we are frustrated. And we are seeking a way out. And we are trying to find a solution.

As Commander in Chief, I am neither a Democrat nor a Republican. The men fighting in Vietnam are simply Americans. Our policy in Vietnam is a national policy. It sprang from every lesson that we've learned in this century.

We fought in the First World War and then we failed to build a system of collective security which could have prevented the Second World War.

Standing in this great city of Chicago, one of our greatest leaders ever to be produced in America, on October 5, 1937, Franklin D. Roosevelt said—and I quote him: "When an epidemic of physical disease starts to spread the community approves and joins in a quarantine of the patient in order to protect the health of the community against the spread of the disease. War is a contagion whether it be declared or undeclared. It can engulf states and peoples remote from the original scene of hostility."

The country heard him, but did not listen.

The country failed to back him in that trying hour. And then we saw what happened when the aggressors felt confident that they could win while we sat by.

That was what President Truman remembered in 1947 in Greece and Turkey. That is what he remembered during the blockade of Berlin and when the attack came in Korea.

That is what President Eisenhower remembered in 1954 when he laid before the Senate the SEATO treaty and during the crisis over Quemoy and Matsu.

That is what President John F. Kennedy remembered when in the face of Communist aggression in Laos and Vietnam he began to send American forces there as early as 1962.

Yes, we have learned over the past half-century that failure to meet aggression means war, not peace. In carrying out that policy we have taken casualties in Berlin and Korea and now in Vietnam. We have had 160,000 American casualties from World War II up until Vietnam. Now every morning I look at those casualty figures. I measure them not as statistics, but man by man. As of this morning we lost 1,705 Americans in Vietnam in the year 1966—1,705—but we lost 49,000 last year on our highways.

And I tell you that if we fail in frustrating this aggression the war that would surely come in Asia would produce casualties not in the 1700s but in the hundreds of thousands and perhaps in millions.

Your government, therefore, under your President, is determined to resist this aggression at the minimum cost to our people and to our allies and to the world.

I don't know what true men may be trying to influence and I do not seek to influence any tonight. But I do tell you here and now that we do not seek to enlarge this war, but we shall not run out on it!

America is determined to meet her commitments tonight because those commitments are right. As I said after a meeting yesterday with Ambassador Lodge just as he was returning to his post of duty, we shall continue to struggle against aggression and social misery in South Vietnam. We shall use our influence to help this young nation come together and move toward constitutional govern-ment. We shall seek an honorable peace.

Let those, though, who speak and write about Vietnam say clearly what other policy they would pursue, and let them weigh their words carefully—let them remember that tonight there are 300,000 young Americans—our own boys—out there somewhere in Southeast Asia on the land and on the sea, and in the air, they are there fighting to quarantine another aggressor, they are there fighting for the peace of the world, and let them remember that there are men on the other side who know well that their only hope for success in this aggression lies in a weakening of the fiber and the determination of the people of America.

And so long as I am President the policy of opposing aggression at minimum cost shall be continued!

I sent our ambassadors to more than forty countries. I wrote letters to nearly 120 in the world asking for assistance, asking for peace. My plea was well received in all the nations of the world except the two most concerned—Red China and North Vietnam. After thirty-seven long days, while our men in uniform waited and while our planes were grounded on my orders, while our ambassadors went from nation to nation, we finally were forced to the conclusion that the time had not yet arrived when the government of North Vietnam was willing or could even be persuaded to sit down at a peace table and try to reason these problems out.

Therefore, our arguments need to be more persuasive and our determinations need to be more convincing and more compelling than they have been. All I can say to you tonight is that the road ahead is going to be difficult.

There will be some Nervous Nellies and some who will become frustrated and bothered and break ranks under the strain. And some will turn on their leaders and on their country and on our own fighting men. There will be times of trial and tensions in the days ahead that will exact the best that is in all of us.

But I have not the slightest doubt that the courage and the dedi-cation and the good sense of the wise American people will ulti-mately prevail. They will stand united until every boy is brought home safely, until the gallant people of South Vietnam have their own choice of their own government.

More than that, not just that one little country of 14 million people but more than a hundred other little countries stand tonight and watch and wait. If America's commitment is dishonored in South

Vietnam, it is dishonored in forty other alliances or more that we have made. So I leave you with the assurance that we love peace and we seek it every hour of every day.

Any person who wishes to test us can give us the time and the date and the place and he will find us occupying our peace chair at the negotiating table with any government who genuinely and who sincerely wants to talk instead of fight.

Perhaps my sentiments and my feelings are best expressed by the words of President Roosevelt when he prepared only a day or so before he died in 1945 this speech and he never had an opportunity to deliver it. He said: "We seek peace, enduring peace. More than an end to war, we want an end to the beginnings of all wars. Yes, an end to this brutal, inhuman and thoroughly impractical method of settling the differences between governments. . . ."

The men who fight for us out there tonight in Vietnam, they are trying to find a way to peace.

But they know, and I don't understand why we don't all recognize, that we can't get peace just for wishing for it. We must get on with the job, until these men can come marching home, some day when peace is secure—not only for the people of America, but peace is secure for peace-loving people everywhere in this world.

Questions

1.   What are the reasons President Johnson gives for fighting in Vietnam? How does he support his reasons?

2.   Is his analogy between deaths in Vietnam and deaths on our highways effective? Is it valid? Of what does he try to convince us with this analogy?

3.   At one point in his speech—in a deviation from his prepared text—Johnson resorts to name-calling. What beliefs do the "Nervous Nellies" probably hold? Has Johnson validated his name-calling by arguing persuasively that those who oppose his policy are weak-kneed and frustrated? How might a Nervous Nellie respond to Johnson's accusations? Might George Wald have been one of these Nervous Nellies?

4.   Compare Johnson's speech with Wald's. One justifies the war; the other condemns it. Which speech is more persuasive and why?

Composition

1.   As a citizen or resident of the United States, you have a right and, indeed, a duty to voice your opinions to the President, the Congress, and to other elected officials. Write a letter to President Johnson (as if he were still President) in which you give your reasons for supporting or opposing the stand he takes in his speech.

2.   Write a letter to one of the men currently in political office, expressing your views on a question that concerns the military and war (for example, Vietnam, involvement in Southeast Asia, the draft, the volunteer army, the ABM controversy, or the power of the Pentagon). When you have finished this letter, you might actually send it.

2. My Lai, March 16, 1968

SEYMOUR M. HERSH

The killings began without warning. Harry Stanley told the C.I.D. that one young member of Calley's platoon took a civilian into custody and then "pushed the man up to where we were standing and then stabbed the man in the back with his bayonet . . . The man fell to the ground and was gasping for breath." The GI then "killed him with another bayonet thrust or by shooting him with a rifle . . . There was so many people killed that day it is hard for me to recall exactly how some of the people died." The youth next "turned to where some soldiers were holding another forty- or fifty-year-old man in custody." He "picked this man up and threw him down a well. Then [he] pulled the pin from a M26 grenade and threw it in after the man." Moments later Stanley saw "some old women and some little children—fifteen or twenty of them—in a group around a temple where some incense was burning. They were kneeling and crying and praying, and various soldiers . . . walked by and executed these women and children by shooting them in the head with their rifles. The soldiers killed all fifteen or twenty of them . . ."

There were few physical protests from the people; about eighty of them were taken quietly from their homes and herded together in the plaza area. A few hollered out, "No VC. No VC." But that was hardly unexpected. Calley left Meadlo, Boyce and a few others with the responsibility of guarding the group. "You know what I want you to do with them," he told Meadlo. Ten minutes later—about 8:15 A.M.—he returned and asked, "Haven't you got rid of them yet? I want them dead." Radioman Sledge, who was trailing Calley, heard the officer tell Meadlo to "waste them." Meadlo followed orders: "We stood about ten to fifteen feet away from them and then he [Calley] started shooting them. Then he told me to start shooting them. I started to shoot them. So we went ahead and killed them. I used more than a whole clip—used four or five clips." There are seventeen M16 bullets in each clip. Boyce slipped away, to the northern side of the hamlet, glad he hadn't been asked to shoot. Women were huddled against their children, vainly trying to save them. Some continued to chant, "No VC." Others simply said, "No. No. No."

Do Chuc is a gnarled forty-eight-year-old Vietnamese peasant whose two daughters and an aunt were killed by the GIs in My Lai 4 that day. He and his family were eating breakfast when the GIs entered the hamlet and ordered them out of their homes. Together with other villagers, they were marched a few hundred meters into the plaza, where they were told to squat. "Still we had no reason to be afraid," Chuc recalled. "Everyone was calm." He watched as the GIs set up a machine gun. The calm ended. The people began crying and begging. One monk showed his identification papers to a soldier, but the American simply said, "Sorry." Then the shooting started. Chuc was wounded in the leg, but he was covered by dead bodies and thus spared. After waiting an hour, he fled the hamlet.

Nguyen Bat, a Viet Cong hamlet chief who later defected, said that many of the villagers who were eating breakfast outdoors when the GIs marched in greeted them without fear. They were gathered together and shot. Other villagers who were breakfasting indoors were killed inside their homes.

The few Viet Cong who had stayed near the hamlet were safely hidden. Nguyen Ngo, a former deputy commander of a Viet Cong guerrilla platoon operating in the My Lai area, ran to his hiding place 300 meters away when the GIs came in shooting, but he could see that "they shot everything in sight." His mother and sister hid in ditches and survived because bodies fell on top of them. Pham Lai, a former hamlet security guard, climbed into a bunker with a

The Third of May, 1808 by Goya. Reproduced by permission of the Prado Museum, Madrid.

bamboo top and heard but did not see the shootings. His wife, hidden under a body, survived the massacre.

By this time, there was shooting everywhere. Dennis I. Conti, a GI from Providence, Rhode Island, later explained to C.I.D. investigators what he thought had happened: "We were all psyched up, and as a result, when we got there the shooting started, almost as a chain reaction. The majority of us had expected to meet VC combat troops, but this did not turn out to be so. First we saw a few men running . . . and the next thing I knew we were shooting at everything. Everybody was just firing. After they got in the village, I guess you could say that the men were out of control."

Brooks and his men in the second platoon to the north had begun to systematically ransack the hamlet and slaughter the people, kill the livestock and destroy the crops. Men poured rifle and machine-gun fire into huts without knowing—or seemingly caring—who was inside.

Roy Wood, one of Calley's men who was working next to Brooks' platoon stormed into a hut, saw an elderly man hiding inside along with his wife and two young daughters: "I hit him with my rifle and pushed him out." A GI from Brooks' platoon, standing by with an M79 grenade launcher, asked to borrow his gun. Wood refused, and the soldier asked another platoon mate. He got the weapon, said, "Don't let none of them live," and shot the Vietnamese in the head. "These mothers are crazy," Wood remembered thinking. "Stand right in front of us and blow a man's brains out." Later he vomited when he saw more of the dead residents of My Lai 4.

The second platoon went into My Lai 4 with guns blazing. Gary Crossley said that some GIs, after seeing nothing but women and children in the hamlet, hesitated: "We phoned Medina and told him what the circumstances were, and he said just keep going. It wasn't anything we wanted to do. You can only kill so many women and children. The fact was that you can't go through and wipe out all of South Vietnam."

Once the first two platoons had disappeared into the hamlet, Medina ordered the third platoon to start moving. He and his men followed. Gary Garfolo was caught up in the confusion: "I could hear heavy shooting all the time. Medina was running back and forth everywhere. This wasn't no organized deal." So Garfolo did what most GIs did when they could get away with it. "I took off on my own." He ran south; others joined him. Terrified villagers, many carrying personal belongings in wicker baskets, were running everywhere to avoid the carnage. In most cases it didn't help. The helicopter gunships circling above cut them down, or else an unfortunate group ran into the third platoon. Charles West sighted and shot six Vietnamese, some with baskets, on the edge of My Lai 4: "These people were running into us, away from us, running every which way. It's hard to distinguish a mama-san from a papa-san when everybody has on black pajamas."

West and his men may have thought that these Vietnamese were Viet Cong. Later they knew better. West's first impression upon reaching My Lai 4: "There were no people in the first part . . . I seen bodies everywhere. I knew that everyone was being killed." His group quickly joined in.

Medina—as any combat officer would do during his unit's first major engagement—decided to move his CP from the rice paddy. John Paul, one of Medina's radiomen, figured that the time was about 8:15 A.M. West remembered that "Medina was right behind us" as his platoon moved inside the hamlet. There are serious contradictions about what happened next. Medina later said that he did not enter the hamlet proper until well after 10 A.M. and did not see anyone kill a civilian. John Paul didn't think that Medina ever entered the hamlet. But Herbert Carter told the C.I.D. that Medina did some of the shooting of civilians as he moved into My Lai 4.

Carter testified that soon after the third platoon moved in, a woman was sighted. Somebody knocked her down, and then, Carter said, "Medina shot her with his M16 rifle. I was fifty or sixty feet away and saw this. There was no reason to shoot this girl." The men continued on, making sure no one was escaping. "We came to where the soldiers had collected fifteen or more Vietnamese men, women and children in a group. Medina said, 'Kill every one. Leave no one standing.'" A machine gunner began firing into the group. Moments later one of Medina's radio operators slowly "passed among them and finished them off." Medina did not personally shoot any of them, according to Carter, but moments later the captain "stopped a seventeen- or eighteen-year-old man with a water buffalo. Medina told the boy to make a run for it," Carter told the C.I.D. "He tried to get him to run but the boy wouldn't run, so Medina shot him with his M16 rifle and killed him . . . I was seventy-five or eighty meters away at the time and I saw it plainly." At this point in Carter's interrogation, the investigator warned him that he was making very serious charges against his commanding officer. "What I'm telling is the truth," Carter replied, "and I'll face Medina in court and swear to it."

If Carter was correct, Medina walked first into the north side of My Lai 4, then moved south with the CP to the hamlet plaza and arrived there at about the time Paul Meadlo and Lieutenant Calley were executing the first group of villagers. Meadlo still wonders why Medina didn't stop the shooting, "if it was wrong." Medina and Calley "passed each other quite a few times that morning, but didn't say anything. I don't know if the CO gave the order to kill or not, but he was right there when it happened . . . Medina just kept marching around."

Roberts and Haeberle also moved in just behind the third platoon. Haeberle watched a group of ten to fifteen GIs methodically pump bullets into a cow until it keeled over. A woman then poked her head out from behind some brush; she may have been hiding in a bunker. The GIs turned their fire from the cow to the woman. "They just kept shooting at her. You could see the bones flying in the air chip by chip." No one had attempted to question her; GIs inside the hamlet also were asking no questions. Before moving on, the photographer took a picture of the dead woman. Haeberle took many more pictures that day; he saw about thirty GIs kill at least a hundred Vietnamese civilians.

When the two correspondents entered My Lai 4, they saw dead animals, dead people, burning huts and houses. A few GIs were going through victims' clothing, looking for piasters. Another GI was chasing a duck with a knife; others stood around watching a GI slaughter a cow with a bayonet.

Haeberle noticed a man and two small children walking toward a group of GIs: "They just kept walking toward us . . . you could hear the little girl saying, 'No, no . . .' All of a sudden the GIs opened up and cut them down." Later he watched a machine gunner suddenly open fire on a group of civilians—women, children and babies—who had been collected in a big circle: "They were trying to run. I don't know how many got out." He saw a GI with an M16 rifle fire at two young boys walking along a road. The older of the two—about seven or eight years old—fell over the first to protect him. The GI kept on firing until both were dead.

As Haeberle and Roberts walked further into the hamlet, Medina came up to them. Eighty-five Viet Cong had been killed in action thus far, the captain told them, and twenty suspects had been captured. Roberts carefully jotted down the captain's statistics in his notepad.

The company's other Vietnamese interpreter, Sergeant Duong Minh, saw Medina for the first time about then. Minh had arrived on a later helicopter assault, along with Lieutenant Dennis H. Johnson, Charlie Company's intelligence officer. When he saw the bodies of civilians, he asked Medina what happened. Medina, obviously angry at Minh for asking the question, stalked away.

Now it was nearly nine o'clock and all of Charlie Company was in My Lai 4. Most families were being shot inside their homes, or just outside the doorways. Those who had tried to flee were crammed by GIs into the many bunkers built throughout the hamlet for protection—once the bunkers became filled, hand grenades were lobbed in. Everything became a target. Gary Garfolo borrowed someone's M79 grenade launcher and fired it point-blank at a water buffalo: "I hit that sucker right in the head; went down like a shot. You don't get to shoot water buffalo with an M79 every day." Others fired the weapons into the bunkers full of people.

Jay Roberts insisted that he saw Medina in My Lai 4 most of the morning: "He was directing the operations in the village. He was in the village the whole time I was—from nine o'clock to eleven o'clock."

Carter recalled that some GIs were shouting and yelling during the massacre: "The boys enjoyed it. When someone laughs and jokes about what they're doing, they have to be enjoying it." A GI said, "Hey, I got me another one." Another said, "Chalk up one for me." Even Captain Medina was having a good time, Carter thought: "You can tell when someone enjoys their work." Few members of Charlie Company protested that day. For the most part, those who didn't like what was going on kept their thoughts to themselves.

Herbert Carter also remembered seeing Medina inside the hamlet well after the third platoon began its advance: "I saw all those dead people laying there. Medina came right behind me." At one point in the morning one of the members of Medina's CP joined in the shooting. "A woman came out of a hut with a baby in her arms and she was crying," Carter told the C.I.D. "She was crying because her little boy had been in front of their hut and . . . someone had killed the child by shooting it." When the mother came into view, one of Medina's men "shot her with an M16 and she fell. When she fell, she dropped the baby." The GI next "opened up on the baby with his M16." The infant was also killed. Carter also saw an officer grab a woman by the hair and shoot her with a .45-caliber pistol: "He held her by the hair for a minute and then let go and she fell to the ground. Some enlisted man standing there said, 'Well, she'll be in the big rice paddy in the sky.' "

In the midst of the carnage, Michael Bernhardt got his first good look at My Lai 4. Bernhardt had been delayed when Medina asked him to check out a suspicious wood box at the landing zone. After discovering that it wasn't a booby trap, Bernhardt hurried to catch up with his mates in the third platoon. He went into the hamlet, where he saw Charlie Company "doing strange things. One: they were setting fire to the hootches and huts and waiting for people to come out and then shooting them. Two: they were going into the hootches and shooting them up. Three: they were gathering people in groups and shooting them. The whole thing was so deliberate. It was point-blank murder and I was standing there watching it. It's kind of made me wonder if I could trust people any more."

Grzesik and his men, meanwhile, had been slowly working their way through the hamlet. The young GI was having problems controlling his men; he was anxious to move on to the rice paddy in the east. About three quarters of the way through, he suddenly saw Meadlo again. The time was now after nine. Meadlo was crouched, head in his hands, sobbing like a bewildered child. "I sat down and asked him what happened." Grzesik felt responsible; after all, he was supposed to be a team leader. Meadlo told him Calley had made him shoot people. "I tried to calm him down," Grzesik said, but the fire-team leader couldn't stay long. His men still hadn't completed their sweep of My Lai 4.

Those Vietnamese who were not killed on the spot were being shepherded by the first platoon to a large drainage ditch at the eastern end of the hamlet. After Grzesik left, Meadlo and a few others gathered seven or eight villagers in one hut and were preparing to toss in a hand grenade when an order came to take them to the ditch. There he found Calley, along with a dozen other first platoon members, and perhaps seventy-five Vietnamese, mostly women, old men and children.

Not far away, invisible in the brush and trees, the second and third platoons were continuing their search-and-destroy operations in the northern half of My Lai 4. Ron Grzesik and his fire team had completed a swing through the hamlet and were getting ready to turn around and walk back to see what was going on. And just south of the plaza, Michael Bernhardt had attached himself to Medina and his command post. Shots were still being fired, the helicopters were still whirring overhead, and the enemy was still nowhere in sight.

One of the helicopters was piloted by Chief Warrant Officer Hugh C. Thompson of Decatur, Georgia. For him, the mission had begun routinely enough. He and his two-man crew, in a small observation helicopter from the 123rd Aviation Battalion, had arrived at the area around 9A.M. and immediately reported what appeared to be a Viet Cong soldier armed with a weapon and heading south. Although his mission was simply reconnaissance, Thompson directed his men to fire at and attempt to kill the Viet Cong as he wheeled the helicopter after him. They missed. Thompson flew back to My Lai 4, and it was then, as he told the Army Inspector General's office in June, 1969, that he began seeing wounded and dead Vietnamese civilians all over the hamlet, with no sign of an enemy force.

The pilot thought that the best thing he could do would be to mark the location of wounded civilians with smoke so that the GIs on the ground could move over and begin treating some of them. "The first one that I marked was a girl that was wounded," Thompson testified, "and they came over and walked up to her, put their weapons on automatic and let her have it." The man who did the shooting was a captain, Thompson said. Later he identified the officer as Ernest Medina.

Flying with Thompson that day was Lawrence M. Colburn, of Mount Vernon, Washington, who remembered that the girl was about twenty years old and was lying on the edge of a dyke outside the hamlet with part of her body in a rice paddy. "She had been wounded in the stomach, I think, or the chest," Colburn told the Inspector General (IG). "This captain was coming down the dyke and he had men behind him. They were sweeping through and we were hovering a matter of feet away from them. I could see this clearly, and he emptied a clip into her."

Medina and his men immediately began moving south toward the Viet Cong sighted by Thompson. En route they saw the young girl in the rice paddy who had been marked by the smoke. Bernhardt had a ground view of what happened next: "He [Medina] was just going alone . . . he shot the woman. She seemed to be busy picking rice, but rice was out of season. What she really was doing was trying to pretend that she was picking rice. She was a hundred meters away with a basket . . . if she had a hand grenade, she would have to have a better arm than me to get us . . . Medina lifted the rifle to his shoulder, looked down the barrel and pulled the trigger. I saw the woman drop. He just took a potshot . . . he wasn't a bad shot. Then he walked up. He got up real close, about three or six feet, and shot at her a couple times and finished her off. She was a real clean corpse . . . she wasn't all over the place, and I could see her clothing move when the bullets hit . . . I could see her twitch, but I couldn't see any holes . . . he didn't shoot her in the head." A second later, Bernhardt remembered, the captain "gave me a look, a dumb shit-eating grin."

By now it was past 9:30 A.M. and the men of Charlie Company had been at work for more than two hours. A few of them flung off their helmets, stripped off their heavy gear, flopped down and took a smoke break.

Questions

1.   In his speech on Vietnam, President Johnson says: "We shall continue to struggle against aggression and social misery in South Vietnam." How might Do Chuc, a survivor of My Lai, respond to this assertion?

2.   Even after William Calley himself and more than a hundred others testified at the Calley trial that American soldiers had killed defenseless civilians, including children and babies, many Americans refused to believe that any wrong had been done. Rallies were held, songs were written, and speeches were made calling Calley a martyr and a hero. The argument went: Calley and the others were just doing their jobs. We should not send those boys out to fight a war and then blame them for killing on the battlefield. Where do you stand on the question?

3.   The killings at My Lai were shocking, not because atrocities are unknown in war, but because Americans committed them. Wanton slaughter, rape, and torture had always been the acts of barbarians. Is there an explanation for these acts implicit in Hersh's narrative? How do you explain them?

Composition

1.   The massacre at My Lai was almost certainly unpremeditated, but the seeds for it must have been planted long before the troops reached the hamlet. Write an essay in which you discuss the planting of the seeds for My Lai 4. Was it army training or the nature of the war? Or do the sources of violence go deeper and reach back into aspects of American culture and society? Draw on your own experience. Look closely at the things around you. Test their culpability.

3. Notes and Comments from The New Yorker

GEORGE WALD'S ''A GENERATION IN SEARCH OF A FUTURE''

On Tuesday, March 4th, in the Kresge Auditorium at the Massachusetts Institute of Technology, a group of scientists assembled, with students and others, to discuss the uses of scientific knowledge. There is nothing we might print in these columns that could be more urgent than the extemporaneous speech, made before that gathering by George Wald, professor of biology at Harvard and Nobel Prize winner, under the title "A Generation in Search of a Future." We therefore quote from it here at length:

"All of you know that in the last couple of years there has been student unrest; breaking at times into violence, in many parts of the world: in England, Germany, Italy, Spain, Mexico, Japan, and, needless to say, many parts of this country. There has been a great deal of discussion as to what it all means. Perfectly clearly, it means something different in Mexico from what it does in France, and something different in France from what it does in Tokyo, and something different in Tokyo from what it does in this country. Yet, unless we are to assume that students have gone crazy all over the world, or that they have just decided that it's the thing to do, it must have some common meaning.

"I don't need to go so far afield to look for that meaning. I am a teacher, and at Harvard I have a class of about three hundred and fifty students—men and women—most of them freshmen and sophomores. Over these past few years, I have felt increasingly that something is terribly wrong—and this year ever so much more than last. Something has gone sour, in teaching and in learning. It's almost as though there were a widespread feeling that education has become irrelevant.

"A lecture is much more of a dialogue than many of you probably realize. As you lecture, you keep watching the faces, and information keeps coming back to you all the time. I began to feel, particularly this year, that I was missing much of what was coming back. I tried asking the students, but they didn't or couldn't help me very much.

"But I think I know what's the matter. I think that this whole generation of students is beset with a profound uneasiness, and I don't think that they have yet quite defined its source. I think I understand the reasons for their uneasiness even better than they do. What is more, I share their uneasiness.

"What's bothering those students? Some of them tell you it's the Vietnam war. I think the Vietnam war is the most shameful episode in the whole of American history. The concept of war crimes is an American invention. We've committed many war crimes in Vietnam—but I'll tell you something interesting about that. We were committing war crimes in World War II, before the Nuremberg trials were held and the principle of war crimes was stated. The saturation bombing of German cities was a war crime. Dropping those atomic bombs on Hiroshima and Nagasaki was a war crime. If we had lost the war, it might have been *our* leaders who had to answer for such actions. I've gone through all that history lately, and I find that there's a gimmick in it. It isn't written out, but I think we established it by precedent. That gimmick is that if one can allege that one is repelling or retaliating for an aggression, after that everything goes.

"And, you see, we are living in a world in which all wars are wars of defense. All War Departments are now Defense Departments. This is all part of the doubletalk of our time. The aggressor is always on the other side. I suppose this is why our ex-Secretary of State Dean Rusk went to such pains to insist, as he still insists, that in Vietnam we are repelling an aggression. And if that's what we are doing—so runs the doctrine—everything goes. If the concept of war crimes is ever to mean anything, they will have to be defined as categories of *acts,* regardless of alleged provocation. But that isn't so now.

"I think we've lost that war, as a lot of other people think, too. The Vietnamese have a secret weapon. It's their willingness to die beyond our willingness to kill. In effect, they've been saying, You can kill us, but you'll have to kill a lot of us; you may have to kill all of us. And, thank heaven, we are not yet ready to do that.

"Yet we have come a long way toward it—far enough to sicken many Americans, far enough to sicken even our fighting men. Far enough so that our national symbols have gone sour. How many of you can sing about 'the rockets' red glare, the bombs bursting in air' without thinking, Those are *our* bombs and *our* rockets, bursting over South Vietnamese villages? When those words were written, we were a people struggling for freedom against oppression. Now we are supporting open or thinly disguised military dictatorships all over the world, helping them to control and repress peoples struggling for their freedom.

"But that Vietnam war, shameful and terrible as it is, seems to me only an immediate incident in a much larger and more stubborn situation.

"Part of my trouble with students is that almost all the students I teach were born after World War II. Just after World War II, a series of new and abnormal procedures came into American life. We regarded them at the time as temporary aberrations. We thought we would get back to normal American life someday.

"But those procedures have stayed with us now for more than twenty years, and those students of mine have never known anything else. They think those things are normal. They think that we've always had a Pentagon, that we have always had a big Army, and that we have always had a draft. But those are all new things in American life, and I think that they are incompatible with what America meant before.

"How many of you realize that just before World War II the entire American Army, including the Air Corps, numbered a hundred and thirty-nine thousand men? Then World War II started, but we weren't yet in it, and, seeing that there was great trouble in the world, we doubled this Army to two hundred and sixty-eight thousand men. Then, in World War II, it got to be eight million. And then World War II came to an end and we prepared to go back to a peacetime Army, somewhat as the American Army had always been before. And, indeed, in 1950—you think about 1950, our international commitments, the Cold War, the Truman Doctrine, and all the rest of it—in 1950, we got down to six hundred thousand men.

"Now we have three and a half million men under arms: about six hundred thousand in Vietnam, about three hundred thousand more in 'support areas' elsewhere in the Pacific, about two hundred and fifty thousand in Germany. And there are a lot at home. Some months ago, we were told that three hundred thousand National Guardsmen and two hundred thousand reservists—so half a million men—had been specially trained for riot duty in the cities.

"I say the Vietnam war is just an immediate incident because as long as we keep that big an Army, it will always find things to do. If the Vietnam war stopped tomorrow, the chances are that with that big a military establishment we would be in another such adventure, abroad or at home, before you knew it.

"The thing to do about the draft is not to reform it but to get rid of it.

"A peacetime draft is the most un-American thing I know. All the time I was growing up, I was told about oppressive Central European countries and Russia, where young men were forced into the Army, and I was told what they did about it. They chopped off a finger, or shot off a couple of toes, or, better still, if they could manage it, they came to this country. And we understood that, and sympathized, and were glad to welcome them.

"Now, by present estimates, from four to six thousand Americans of draft age have left this country for Canada, two or three thousand more have gone to Europe, and it looks as though many more were preparing to emigrate.

"A bill to stop the draft was recently introduced in the Senate (S. 503), sponsored by a group of senators that runs the gamut from McGovern and Hatfield to Barry Goldwater. I hope it goes through. But I think that when we get rid of the draft we must also drastically cut back the size of the armed forces.

"Yet there is something ever so much bigger and more important than the draft. That bigger thing, of course, is the militarization of our country. Ex-President Eisenhower, in his farewell address, warned us of what he called the military-industrial complex. I am sad to say that we must begin to think of it now as the military-industrial-labor-union complex. What happened under the plea of the Cold War was not alone that we built up the first big peacetime Army in our history but that we institutionalized it. We built, I suppose, the biggest government building in our history to run it, and we institutionalized it.

"I don't think we can live with the present military establishment, and its eighty-billion-dollar-a-year budget, and keep America anything like the America we have known in the past. It is corrupting the life of the whole country. It is buying up everything in sight: industries, banks, investors, scientists—and lately it seems also to have bought up the labor unions.

"The Defense Department is always broke, but some of the things it does with that eighty billion dollars a year would make Buck Rogers envious. For example, the Rocky Mountain Arsenal, on the outskirts of Denver, was manufacturing a deadly nerve poison on such a scale that there was a problem of waste disposal. Nothing daunted, the people there dug a tunnel two miles deep under Denver, into which they have injected so much poisoned water that, beginning a couple of years ago, Denver has experienced a series of earth tremors of increasing severity. Now there is grave fear of a major earthquake. An interesting debate is in progress as to whether Denver will be safer if that lake of poisoned water is removed or is left in place.

"Perhaps you have read also of those six thousand sheep that suddenly died in Skull Valley, Utah, killed by another nerve poison —a strange and, I believe, still unexplained accident, since the nearest testing seems to have been thirty miles away.

"As for Vietnam, the expenditure of firepower there has been frightening. Some of you may still remember Khe Sanh, a hamlet just south of the Demilitarized Zone, where a force of United States Marines was beleaguered for a time. During that period, we dropped on the perimeter of Khe Sanh more explosives than fell on Japan throughout World War II, and more than fell on the whole of Europe during the years 1942 and 1943.

"One of the officers there was quoted as having said afterward, 'It looks like the world caught smallpox and died.'

"The only point of government is to safeguard and foster life. Our government has become preoccupied with death, with the business of killing and being killed. So-called defense now absorbs sixty per cent of the national budget, and about twelve per cent of the Gross National Product.

"A lively debate is beginning again on whether or not we should deploy antiballistic missles, the ABM. I don't have to talk about them—everyone else here is doing that. But I should like to mention a curious circumstance. In September, 1967, or about a year and a half ago, we had a meeting of M.I.T. and Harvard people, including experts on these matters, to talk about whether anything could be done to block the Sentinel system—the deployment of ABMs. Everyone present thought them undesirable, but a few of the most knowledgeable persons took what seemed to be the practical view: 'Why fight about a dead issue? It has been decided, the funds have been appropriated. Let's go on from there.'

"Well, fortunately, it's not a dead issue.

"An ABM is a nuclear weapon. It takes a nuclear weapon to stop a nuclear weapon. And our concern must be with the whole issue of nuclear weapons.

"There is an entire semantics ready to deal with the sort of thing I am about to say. It involves such phrases as 'Those are the facts of life.' No—these are the facts of death. I don't accept them, and I advise you not to accept them. We are under repeated pressure to accept things that are presented to us as settled—decisions that have been made. Always there is the thought: Let's go on from there. But this time we don't see how to go on. We will have to stick with these issues.

"We are told that the United States and Russia, between them, by now have stockpiled nuclear weapons of approximately the explosive power of fifteen tons of TNT for every man, woman, and child on earth. And now it is suggested that we must make more. All very regrettable, of course, but 'those are the facts of life.' We really would like to disarm, but our new Secretary of Defense has made the ingenious proposal that now is the time to greatly increase our nuclear armaments, so that we can disarm from a position of strength.

"I think all of you know there is no adequate defense against massive nuclear attack. It is both easier and cheaper to circumvent any known nuclear-defense system than to provide it. It's all pretty crazy. At the very moment we talk of deploying ABMs, we are also building the MIRV, the weapon to circumvent ABMs.

"As far as I know, the most conservative estimates of the number of Americans who would be killed in a major nuclear attack, with everything working as well as can be hoped and all foreseeable precautions taken, run to about fifty million. We have become callous to gruesome statistics, and this seems at first to be only another gruesome statistic. You think, Bang!—and next morning, if you're still there, you read in the newspapers that fifty million people were killed.

"But that isn't the way it happens. When we killed close to two hundred thousand people with those first, little, old-fashioned uranium bombs that we dropped on Hiroshima and Nagasaki, about the same number of persons were maimed, blinded, burned, poisoned, and otherwise doomed. A lot of them took a long time to die.

"That's the way it would be. Not a bang and a certain number of corpses to bury but a nation filled with millions of helpless, maimed, tortured, and doomed persons, and the survivors huddled with their families in shelters, with guns ready to fight off their neighbors trying to get some uncontaminated food and water.

"A few months ago, Senator Richard Russell, of Georgia, ended a speech in the Senate with the words 'If we have to start over again with another Adam and Eve, I want them to be Americans; and I want them on this continent and not in Europe.' That was a United States senator making a patriotic speech. Well, here is a Nobel laureate who thinks that those words are criminally insane.

"How real is the threat of full-scale nuclear war? I have my own very inexpert idea, but, realizing how little I know, and fearful that I may be a little paranoid on this subject, I take every opportunity to ask reputed experts. I asked that question of a distinguished professor of government at Harvard about a month ago. I asked him what sort of odds he would lay on the possibility of full-scale nuclear war within the foreseeable future. 'Oh,' he said comfortably, 'I think I can give you a pretty good answer to that question. I estimate the probability of full-scale nuclear war, provided that the situation remains about as it is now, at two per cent per year.' Anybody can do the simple calculation that shows that two percent per year means that the chance of having that full-scale nuclear war by 1990 is about one in three, and by 2000 it is about fifty-fifty.

"I think I know what is bothering the students. I think that what we are up against is a generation that is by no means sure that it has a future.

"I am growing old, and my future, so to speak, is already behind me. But there are those students of mine, who are in my mind always; and there are my children, the youngest of them now seven and nine, whose future is infinitely more precious to me than my own. So it isn't just their generation; it's mine, too. We're all in it together.

"Are we to have a chance to live? We don't ask for prosperity, or security. Only for a reasonable chance to live, to work out our destiny in peace and decency. Not to go down in history as the apocalyptic generation.

"And it isn't only nuclear war. Another overwhelming threat is in the population explosion. That has not yet even begun to come under control. There is every indication that the world population will double before the year 2000, and there is a widespread expectation of famine on an unprecedented scale in many parts of the world. The experts tend to differ only in their estimates of when those famines will begin. Some think by 1980; others think they can be staved off until 1990; very few expect that they will not occur by the year 2000.

"That is the problem. Unless we can be surer than we now are that this generation has a future, nothing else matters. It's not good enough to give it tender, loving care, to supply it with breakfast foods, to buy it expensive educations. Those things don't mean anything unless this generation has a future. And we're not sure that it does.

"I don't think that there are problems of youth, or student problems. All the real problems I know about are grown-up problems.

"Perhaps you will think me altogether absurd, or 'academic,' or hopelessly innocent—that is, until you think of the alternatives—if I say, as I do to you now: We have to get rid of those nuclear weapons. There is nothing worth having that can be obtained by nuclear war— nothing material or ideological—no tradition that it can defend. It is utterly self-defeating. Those atomic bombs represent an unusable weapon. The only use for an atomic bomb is to keep somebody else from using one. It can give us no protection—only the doubtful satisfaction of retaliation. Nuclear weapons offer us nothing but a balance of terror, and a balance of terror is still terror.

"We have to get rid of those atomic weapons, here and everywhere. We cannot live with them.

"I think we've reached a point of great decision, not just for our nation, not only for all humanity, but for life upon the earth. I tell my students, with a feeling of pride that I hope they will share, that the carbon, nitrogen, and oxygen that make up ninety-nine per cent of our living substance were cooked in the deep interiors of earlier generations of dying stars. Gathered up from the ends of the universe, over billions of years, eventually they came to form, in part, the substance of our sun, its planets, and ourselves. Three billion years ago, life arose upon the earth. It is the only life in the solar system.

"About two million years ago, man appeared. He has become the dominant species on the earth. All other living things, animal and plant, live by his sufferance. He is the custodian of life on earth, and in the solar system. It's a big responsibility.

"The thought that we're in competition with Russians or with Chinese is all a mistake, and trivial. We are one species, with a world to win. There's life all over this universe, but the only life in the solar system is on earth, and in the whole universe we are the only men.

"Our business is with life, not death. Our challenge is to give what account we can of what becomes of life in the solar system, this corner of the universe that is our home; and, most of all, what becomes of men—all men, of all nations, colors, and creeds. This has become one world, a world for all men. It is only such a world that can now offer us life, and the chance to go on."

"LET'S NOT SPOIL A GOOD THING."

Cartoon by Bill Mauldin Copyright © 1969 The Chicago Sun-Times, *reproduced by courtesy of Wil-Jo Associates, Inc., and Bill Mauldin.*

Mauldin's cartoon says some of the things that Wald says in his speech. Whose statement about the military-industrial-labor union complex is more effective and why?

Mauldin of the *Chicago Sun-Times* and Herblock of the *Washington Post* are two of today's foremost political cartoonists. For a term paper, choose one of these men or another well-known cartoonist and, using his work as your primary source, analyze and discuss his political philosophy.

Questions

1. Why does Wald say: "A peacetime draft is the most un-American thing I know"? Do you agree with him?

2. Recently at the Pentagon a phrase of uncertain origin came into being. During a discussion of American bombing of North Vietnam, an air attack on a missle site was described as a "pre-emptive retaliatory strike." What does this phrase mean? Are we living in an age of "double-talk," as Wald says? Is there anything in the Johnson speech that Wald might call double-talk?

3. What is Wald's attitude toward those who leave the United States to avoid the draft? What is your attitude? Discuss the proposals of some congressmen to make a treaty with Canada that would assure the return of these men.

4. Why does Wald say that under present conditions we will always have a Vietnam or "another such adventure, abroad or at home"? Why does he include "at home"? Does he give concrete evidence that problems stemming from the war have already developed in the United States? What must be done to avoid such disasters?

5. What use does Wald make of statistics? What does he do to the figures to sharpen their sense of reality?

6. Why does he call Richard Russell's comments "criminally insane"? Do you agree with him?

7. How would you describe the persona or voice who delivers this speech? Does Wald make good use of the fact that he is a Nobel laureate? What is his relationship to his audience?

8. The massacre at My Lai occurred on March 16, 1968, almost a year before Wald's speech. Knowledge of the massacre was not general, however, until late 1969. Can you infer from his speech what Wald's response to the news of My Lai would be?

Composition

1. You have all seen bumper stickers on cars which read: "America: Love It or Leave It." Write an essay in which you tell what it means to love America today. As an alternative assign-

ment, write an essay in which you discuss this bumper slogan as a manifestation of a common way of thinking in America. Would you call the attitudes of people who think this way healthy or unhealthy?

2.   Faced with the call to serve in the armed forces, would you fight in Vietnam or, if you are not facing military service, would you urge, however reluctantly, your fiancé, husband, or brother to fight? In responding to this problem, assume that you are addressing someone or some group that is opposed to your stand but is willing to listen fairly to your case.

4. The Defence of Fort M'Henry

FRANCIS SCOTT KEY

O! say can you see, by the dawn's early light,
What so proudly we hail'd at the twilight's last gleaming,
Whose broad stripes and bright stars through the perilous fight,
O'er the ramparts we watch'd, were so gallantly streaming?
And the rockets' red glare, the bombs bursting in air,
Gave proof through the night that our flag was still there . . .
O! say, does that star-spangled banner yet wave
O'er the land of the free, and the home of the brave?

On the shore, dimly seen through the mists of the deep,
Where the foe's haughty host in dread silence reposes,
What is that which the breeze o'er the towering steep,
As it fitfully blows, half conceals, half discloses?
Now it catches the gleam of the morning's first beam,
In full glory reflected now shines on the stream—
'Tis the star-spangled banner, O! long may it wave
O'er the land of the free, and the home of the brave.

And where is that band who so vauntingly swore
That the havock of war and the battle's confusion
A home and a country should leave us no more?
Their blood has wash'd out their foul foot-steps' pollution.
No refuge could save the hireling and slave,

From the terror of flight or the gloom of the grave;
And the star-spangled banner in triumph doth wave
O'er the land of the free, and the home of the brave.

O! thus be it ever when freemen shall stand
Between their lov'd home, and the war's desolation,
Blest with vict'ry and peace, may the heav'n rescued land
Praise the power that hath made and preserv'd us a nation!
Then conquer we must, when our cause it is just,
And this be our motto—"In God is our trust!"
And the star-spangled banner in triumph shall wave
O'er the land of the free, and the home of the brave.

Questions

1. Known also as "The Star-Spangled Banner" this lyric, set to music, is the national anthem of the United States. Discuss the appropriateness of the lyric as a symbol of America. Do the words speak honestly and meaningfully of what America is to you? Are war and battle proper subjects for the American national anthem?

2. Why does George Wald say in his speech at M.I.T. that many Americans today have trouble singing the National Anthem? Is he right? Do you have trouble singing this song?

3. The first stanza is made up of two questions, and the second stanza begins with a question. Where and how are these questions answered?

4. Lines 29 and 30 of this poem have often been quoted and paraphrased by politicians and patriots. Do these lines express a truth?

5. In stanza three, the speaker justifies the carnage of war. When and why is this carnage justified? What are your own feelings on the question? What makes a "just" war?

Composition

1. Try writing a film scenario for a realistic visual accompaniment to the first two stanzas.

2. A film by Dan McLauglin called "The Star-Spangled Banner" (1968) juxtaposes in swift succession historical images and a series of shots of the 1968 Chicago riots during the Democratic Convention. As these images flash on the screen—most of them for less than a second—the National Anthem is played in the background. The combination of visual images and sound makes an ironic, nonverbal comment on American ideals and American life. Try something similar. Collect a series of sixty or seventy still images and arrange them in a sequence that can be shown to the accompaniment of "The Star-Spangled Banner." Organize the images so that they make a comment, ironic or not, about American ideals and life. If possible, put the sequence on moving-picture film.